The Globalist Papers

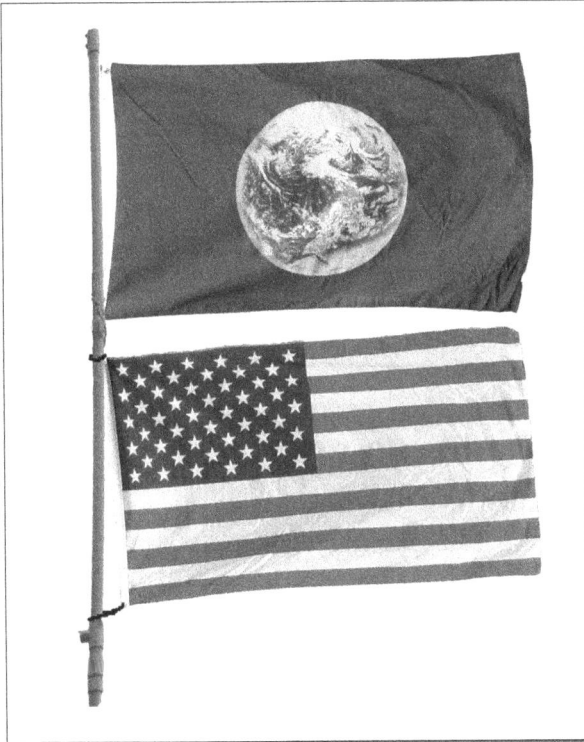

Samuel Avery
Louisville, Kentucky

Special thanks to Bonnie, John, Joanne, Margaret, Judy, Scott, Martha, Joanie, Suzie, Blaire, and Laura.

ISBN-13: 978-0-9741976-1-6
ISBN-10: 0-9741976-1-0

Contents

Part 1 — The Inevitable

1. The Crisis

I WILL PROPHESY WHAT EVERYONE ALREADY KNOWS. I WILL foretell what we all see but do not realize: A crisis will come to the world and all the world will know it at one time. Each will see death in his own heart and in those around him and will die to what he has been. Each will see the death of the world in his own hand. Death will come in that hour, death and the chance of new life. The old life will pass.

I prophesy this because I know that it will happen — today, tomorrow, fifty years from now, or farther into the future. I know it through the sort of prophetic vision one gains by throwing dice repeatedly. It will happen not to fulfill the prophecy, but to reveal in the fullness of time what already is. It is the future built into the present. Everyone knows that it will come, but few allow themselves to realize it. It is time to speak of where we are headed.

War is built into the divisions of humanity. It will come in time. A nuclear war among nations will come in time. It is inevitable. Peace in a world of separate sovereign powers is a temporary condition between wars, a temporary balance of national interests that are represented and enforced by military power. It is a peace built on potential war. A nation is powerful in a divided world by virtue of its preparation for war. Its influence is in proportion to its capacity to kill large numbers of people. A sustained balance of power and lasting peace among independent nations is possible only in a world of static power relations, and that is not the world we live in. In the real world, power relations are readjusted periodically through warfare. Nations whose interests are not adequately represented by potential war resort to actual war.

This has been true throughout history, and there is nothing different about it now. What is different now is the magnitude of potential violence built into power relations. Nations are able to kill many more people than ever before. Until the middle of the twentieth century, the balance of power was adjusted periodically through actualized violence that did not interrupt the continuity of civilization as a whole. War was possible within the context of civilization. Thousands or millions were killed and wounded, thousands or millions robbed and raped and left homeless, whole countries laid waste — but life went on; millions were *not* killed, wounded, or left homeless. There were places in the world that were untouched by war and from which civilization could regenerate itself. The difference now is that these untouched places no longer exist. Civilization will no longer be able to grow back and reestablish itself. Political division remains, the balance of power remains, and the need to adjust the balance of power remains. But the earth is no longer large enough for weapons that nations now have, and there will be no recovery from a major adjustment in the international balance of power. We all know this, but we do not yet allow ourselves to realize it. It is not pleasant to think about, and we prefer not to believe that it is true.

The first nuclear crisis may not be one of general war among major nuclear powers. More likely, it will arise among smaller nuclear powers or between a nuclear nation and a terrorist group with access to nuclear devices. Nuclear weapons are more available every year to smaller nations and to terrorist or separatist movements within nations. Stateless terror groups operate by the same general principle as nation–states: The ability to kill large numbers of people is the ability to be seen and heard on the international stage. They have learned that it is possible to project power through mass violence without armies or formal weaponry.

The potential to create violence commands the attention of adversaries, which is what power is. Nuclear weapons are the greatest source of potential violence and will almost certainly be involved in the coming crisis. The first crisis may or may not destroy civilization, but it when it comes, everyone living will see the destruction of civilization within the immediate range of human will.

At the moment of crisis we will act according to who we think we are. The fear and violence of the moment will show us who we are divided and who we are united. If we understand ourselves to be a *type* of humanity, we will act to defend ourselves from other types. We will defend national interest at the expense of human interest. If, on the other hand, we understand ourselves to be human first and national second, we will become in that moment what we could not be before. The terror of *nonbeing* will speak to us and dare us to become what we can become in no other way. We will act one way or the other according to who we understand ourselves to be and become from then on what we make of ourselves at that moment.

What is meant by human unity, and how is it possible? Unity does not mean the abolition of national government; it means the abolition of national sovereignty. Sovereignty is ultimate political power. The United States, Togo, Zimbabwe, and France are all sovereign powers. Shansi, California, Bavaria, and New South Wales are not. Individuals live within multiple layers of subordinate government (provincial, state, county, township, or municipal), but there can be only one layer of sovereign government, almost always at the national level. The individual's ultimate allegiance is to the sovereignty. He may feel great pride in his hometown or the province where he lives, but he is not expected to kill or die for it. The sovereignty will, in fact, prevent him from doing so. Sovereign governments always suppress conflict among their subordinate governments. They also suppress violence among individuals (though they often cede this right to subordinates), and they always retain the exclusive right to defend against — or to attack — external powers. A sovereign government is, therefore, a monopoly of violence. It may legally kill or threaten to kill either inside or outside its borders, and it will prevent anyone else from attempting to do so. Human unity means a transfer of sovereignty from the national to the global level — and thereby the subordination of national governments to global interests — but it does not mean the glossing over of human differences or the denial of diversity. It does not mean the end of nationality. It means a transfer of primary allegiance of all people from nationality to humanity as a whole. National identity and national government will remain, but the right of the individual to kill or die for his country will be gone forever.

Transfer of sovereignty is usually violent. It is rarely a matter of rational deliberation. Persuasion may be a factor, but sovereignty cannot be transferred through persuasion alone. There must be fear. A prevailing force must threaten death for sovereignty to shift from one community to another. Violence is not actualized in every case — it is often merely threatened — but the threat usually involves its actualization to some extent. The full meaning of violence is not easily appreciated in potential form and in most cases must be shown. The proportion of actual to potential violence is related to how well the situation is understood.

The enormous violence of nuclear weaponry will approach actualization during the upcoming crisis, and the psychology of sovereignty will come to the surface. We will all see it. More important, we will all feel it. At the point of actualization, or shortly thereafter, sovereignty will flow in one direction or another. Conscious awareness may divert the flow of sovereignty to creative channels.

If actual violence is kept to a minimum, humanity will survive the crisis. But if sovereignty flows back into separate nations, the crisis will recur. If and when, after a crisis or series of crises, sovereignty is transferred successfully from the national to the global level, there will be a means of suppressing international warfare, and the crisis will not recur. A rational understanding of the fear we experience together will forge us into something we are not now, and there will be no more war between nations.

Global sovereignty will become a permanent structure of world peace. It will also become a means of addressing other world problems that national governments are incapable of handling effectively. A global government will become a uniform network of international law enforcement, and a worldwide means of supervising and controlling fissile and other weapons-grade materials. International peacekeeping and disaster relief forces, established on a permanent standby basis will be available for nations experiencing civil unrest or natural disaster. Medical, financial, educational, and economic development resources will be channeled to areas where they are most needed rather than distributed in response to the interests of donor nations. Uniform labor and environmental legislation will provide an even playing field for workers and international businesses. The consumption of world resources will be more easily regulated in a fair and even-handed manner, and the health of the atmosphere, oceans, forests, and agricultural lands will be more uniformly monitored and more effectively maintained. Unity will make it possible for human civilization to survive the threat it poses to itself and to meet the challenges of the twenty-first century. Even without the inevitability of nuclear war, a lack of unity would almost certainly lead to the failure of humanity sometime in the next hundred years. The crisis will produce an immediate and visible need for global sovereignty, which will in turn provide the longer-range tools required for human survival.

Despite its necessity and inevitability, global unity will be resisted stubbornly. The nation–state remains the prevailing paradigm, impractical and obsolete as it may be. Nationality is deeply ingrained in how we understand ourselves in relation to organized society, and it is a difficult concept for most people to think around. Most do not question ultimate allegiance to national government and understand the nation and not the world to be the proper object of individual altruism. Thinking people agree, for the most part, that a united world is preferable to a divided world but consider unity impractical because it violates the paradigm. Global unity remains an ideal, a fantasy. Thinking stops inside the "box" of national sovereignty. Those who believe in global unity seem naive, unpatriotic, and treasonous in times of national emergency. The ethereal altruism of global interest seems distant and otherworldly compared to the more immediate altruism of national interest. Until the paradigm changes, the conflict will grow, with supporters of each interest seeing themselves as supporters of the greater good. Each will live by the logic of its own frame of reference and wonder how the other could so plainly mislead and be misled. The conflict will be bitter at times and possibly violent, but will signal that the paradigm has begun to shift. The shift will continue up until — and through — the crisis.

Every nation will suffer political convulsions as its citizens undergo the shift from national to human identity. Some will experience more difficulty than others and resist by force of arms. Others will welcome the benefits of interdependence. The nation with the most to lose and the most to gain will be the United States. As the most powerful and most successful of the modern nation–states, it is the exemplar, par excellence, of the prevailing paradigm. Since the end of the Cold War, it has enjoyed the role of uncontested "superpower." What America does must be taken seriously by everyone, and no other single nation can keep it from doing as it pleases on the world stage. Americans are respected — or feared — by all other peoples in the world. This is the consummate goal of nationalism, and Americans will savor it for as long as it lasts.

But while America enjoys an elevated status in the world, it does not understand itself to be an imperial power and does not care to police the world on an ongoing basis. It sees itself as first among equals: separate, independent, and unburdened by responsibility for the rest of the world. It wants only the global responsibility it chooses for itself. It defines its own missions in the world and usually projects itself with the intention of retracting on completion of the task at hand. America does not believe in global unity and perceives the trend in that direction to be a threat. It participates in international organizations only to the extent that they do not infringe on national sovereignty, and it supports international initiatives only when they coincide with its own particular interests.

Despite America's anti-imperialist self-image and strong sense of independence, it is being sucked into a growing power vacuum on the global level. It is the world's only effective global power and is in danger of becoming, willingly or not, something of a global sovereignty. The new realities of global trade, transportation, communications, and the intercontinental scale of modern weaponry already require the implementation of law and order on the supranational level. Crises in the Middle East, the Balkans, sub-Saharan Africa, the Caribbean, or the Far East command the attention of the whole world and cry out for order and justice. In the absence of an effective permanent peacekeeping force, the world turns to America, and America is forced to respond, whether or not intervention is within its "national interest." The formation of an independent state of Palestine, a rebellion in Liberia, despotism in Iraq, and a nuclear weapons program in North Korea are all thrown at the doorstep of America. These are the types of situations that a global power responds to and the means by which it becomes a global empire. America will become a de facto global empire if it continues to take upon itself the role of preventing other nations from developing nuclear and other weapons of mass destruction.

As disastrous as a global empire would be for America and for the world, it may be the direction in which we are now headed. It is the mostly likely alternative to a democratic global government. It is likely to occur in the *absence* of a conscious paradigm shift; that is, in the absence of the realization that human beings should be united and equal. An American Empire would not *be* a nation–state, but it may evolve incrementally *within* the nation–state paradigm as the survival imperative of global unity becomes apparent. It may evolve as an extension of national power by the most powerful of nations, and thereby become a global unity within a national sovereignty. An imperial America would not sit well in the conscience of the American people and would never be accepted by other nations, but it will happen if people do not see it coming. It may happen without many Americans realizing that it is happening. The trend toward American empire will continue in the period leading to a nuclear crisis, and resistance to it may well provoke that crisis.

If an American empire can be avoided, disproportional American influence in a sovereign global society cannot. America will be bigger in a united world than Russia, China, India, or a united Europe. This will be resented by many, but is an inevitable consequence of American economic, cultural, and military power. The America experience will provide models for the formation and growth of world institutions, and much of what has happened in the course of its history will be of vital significance in the formation of an effective global government. Americans seem naïve and self-absorbed to many non-Americans, but the world admires what America believes about itself, and what it believes about itself is applicable to the rest of the world. Its Declaration of Independence defines the purposes of government generally and the fundamental right of people everywhere to change government. The conscious formation of the federal union through a written constitution demonstrates a means by which sovereign power can be transferred from one level of government to another in a deliberate and bloodless manner. The movement for global unity will incorporate the values and national experiences of people everywhere, but the universality of American ideals, coupled with the global scale of its military power, will mean a unique role for the United States in the formation of a united humanity.

_____

In Part I of this book, I try to show that the trend toward global unity is inevitable. (By *inevitable* I mean *unavoidable*: I do not mean *automatic*.) The scale of political communities (tribe, city–state, nation–state, etc.) is a function of prevailing military technology; the more powerful the weapons become, the larger the states become. Intercontinental weaponry in the current era has made untenable the defense of any portion of the earth's surface against any other. We will not avoid the trend toward global unity no matter what we do; we may avoid its culmination only by avoiding the future altogether.

Part II examines the practical aspects of unity: environmental, economic, and social. Even in the absence of the nuclear imperative, unity will become necessary because independent nation–states are incapable of managing oceanic pollution, climate change, economic development, disease control, globalization of capital and labor markets, population control, and any number of other practical problems of the twenty-first century.

But politics and economics are only the surface of human experience. Part III suggests that unity will come about only with a new spiritual awakening to who we are and what we are doing on Earth. The body of global government cannot exist without its soul.

The papers in Part IV show what can be drawn from the American tradition and applied generally to the world. A united world community will be constructed from the diverse traditions of all peoples, but the American experience with revolution, with violence and disunity, and especially with the creation of a central government from many independent states will be of special significance. America will have the most to gain from world government — and the most to lose.

The process of achieving unity is discussed in Part V. The creation of a global system will require the transfer of sovereignty, a process rarely completed without force of arms. But world peace without oppression cannot be accomplished through violent means. We will look, therefore, at the very few lessons available in our short history of nonviolent social change and apply them to an entirely new and unique situation. Concluding papers are in Part VI.

These papers are not meant to be comprehensive or definitive. I mean only to introduce a general area of inquiry. There are enormous fields of study and interest that I have either touched only lightly or forgotten entirely. Some assertions will be proven wrong; in asserting them I hope only to provoke others to assert that which is right. The particulars are important to the extent of composing a general picture of a divided humanity, despairing of its future and in search of what it will see when it chooses to look. I believe that people are innately creative and capable of reconstituting themselves in an emergency, as some of us were able to do the last time I troubled you with my opinions.

Publius

2. Sovereignty

Political power comes from the barrel of a gun.

— *Mao Ze-dong*

THE STATE IS BUILT BY FEAR. WITHOUT FEAR THERE IS NO political order, and without political order, no human institution is possible. But random fear does not create the state: It must be organized fear. Mao did not mean to have his guns shooting off in all directions; he meant to have them all pointed in the same direction at people he intended to scare. From this government is born.

Mao was not speaking of China or of communism, but of all peoples and all types of political power. Government is organized violence: an organized monopoly of violence. Within a government there can be peace (to the extent that the government governs) and within that peace other forms of organization may arise. Government may perform any number of public functions, but to be government at all it must retain the right — the exclusive right — to use violence within the community and without. It must be prepared to use deadly force against any who challenge this right. All else is built on this principle.

This is a truth that may be tested. If you doubt that it is true, become violent and see what happens. Break into a neighbor's house or begin hitting someone with a stick. If people in uniforms appear on the scene and ask you to stop, ask them why you should do so. They will try to instill fear in you with suggestions of superior physical force. You may test the point further by refusing to stop. If you begin to feel pain, you may soon come to the realization that it is related to the violence you are doing, and you may choose to stop, in which case my point is proven. The government has reclaimed its exclusive right to violence.

If, however, you do not stop, you are demonstrating the government's inability to govern. You become an outlaw. If you demonstrate an ability to inflict violence greater than the government's ability to inflict violence, you become the government. It will be you who provides peace by suppressing the violence of others. The substance of sovereignty will flow through your ability to do the greater damage and through your ability to maintain a monopoly of violence. This is sovereign power.

But more likely, you are a law-abiding citizen and do not choose to become an outlaw or a revolutionary. You do not fear your government in any conscious or immediate sense and are thankful, rather, for the fear it instills in others who *do* challenge its monopoly. You are willing to give up to the government your right to use violence in the hope of gaining protection from those who do not choose to give it up. It is likely that you do not find yourself in the midst of a revolution and are not forced to choose — at the risk of life and liberty — between competing claims to sovereignty and will not experience the fear around which government is built. But you should know that it is there, because when fear is brought to the surface, sovereign relations can change. When people fear for their lives, they can change the very definition of government on its most fundamental level. It is, in fact, the only time they *can* change it.

Over the centuries, sovereignty has flowed through many forms of government — autocracy, oligarchy, monarchy, and democracy — each with its degree of severity and effectiveness. Governments have been fair and responsible, cruel and arbitrary. But it is sovereignty that interests us here, not form or benevolence of government. Sovereignty is the most fundamental context of civil life; particular forms and qualities of authority may occupy that context from time to time, and benevolence may or may not arise once the monopoly of violence is complete. But even a representative and compassionate government must be willing to be violent when necessary: Any form of government cannot exist without government itself. Therefore, if we are to know how new government is to arise among the nations of the earth and how it may be made to serve the interests of those it governs, we should first look at government in its most naked stance and only then clothe it in the manner we prefer.

From what did sovereignty arise, and how did it grow from local to national scale? It is older than written records and older than humanity itself. It existed in its most rudimentary forms among primates and other animals long before people existed, and continues to exist among nonhumans. Among early humans it existed at a personal level as a possession of particular individuals or groups of individuals. Physical strength was its source along with not a little bit of fast talking. It resided in he who could inflict pain on his fellows and who could persuade them to inflict the same on others. He was a bully — but a bully smart enough not to exhaust himself with unnecessary proofs of his powers. He held his energies in reserve, exercising actual violence only to illustrate its potential. He ruled not through fighting but through his reputation as a fighter; he fought only in order to retain the reputation.

But so personal a sovereignty could not be stable for more than a small span of time or cover more than a small number of people. As the reputation of an especially powerful individual spread over time and space, others jealous of the reputation would challenge his exclusive right to do violence. He would lose his monopoly eventually to the superior abilities of some other individual through fighting, accident, or, if he were lucky, through natural aging. Eventually someone else would get away with murder or at least demonstrate the capacity to do so. Sovereignty as a personal possession could not last for more than a few years, and government, such as it was, could not be stable or encompass more than a few square miles or a few dozen individuals.

Government could become stable only through the *institutionalization* of sovereignty. Sovereignty became an abstraction, an idea — a *thing*, however invisible, that permeated the community as a whole, over and above any individual. Its source was beyond the visible world, beyond the here and now, and revealed to the living through myth and ritual. Initiates into civil society were taught from an early age to accept the authority of the group as a whole and of whoever ruled in the name of the group as a whole. The community became not a sum of separate persons, one of whom had risen above the others, but a living organism that could commandeer the talents of the individual for its own purposes. Individuals could exercise sovereignty but not *have* it: The community retained the right to authority as an abstraction superior to the authorized individual. The ruler ruled not out of personal strength but out of legitimacy. Others stronger than the ruler must submit or claim legitimacy for themselves.

The institutionalization of sovereignty stabilized human organizations by creating the possibility for peaceful transfer of authority from one individual to another. The potential for violence became associated with the organic wholeness of the community and therefore could remain un-actualized as it passed from one community member to another. Separate now from the individual, sovereignty became associated with a particular class or family within the community and also with the territory in which the community lived. Challenges to the ruling order or the community's territory were challenges to its sovereignty. In theory, peace in the community was maintained from within through respect of legitimacy and from without through respect of territory. As long as respect prevailed, violence remained potential only. But the system did not depend on goodwill. Challenges

to legitimacy or territory would actualize violence institutional-
ized within the structure of the community and serve to indicate
that the system was working as it should. Punitive law enforcement, dynastic struggles, and the occasional border clash served
to reassure the community that its potential for violence remained
intact.

Once abstracted from the individual, sovereignty could exist
at any level of human organization from local to national and
international. But its flow from one level to another — or from
one territory to another — took place only with an actualization
of potential violence. Individuals understood their lives within the
context of their own sovereign community and were willing to
risk their lives to maintain it. The psychological barrier of shifting
subordination from one sovereign entity to another was as profound as fear for life itself; people would die before allowing the
sovereignty of their community to die. Changes in the scope or
level of sovereignty could occur, therefore, only through warfare.
The institutionalization of sovereignty thus promoted an easy
transfer of power between legitimate individuals within a sovereign entity, but it necessitated actual violence for the shift of sovereignty between levels or territories.

Governments experience a dynamic of continuing pressure on
their sovereign legitimacy both from within and without. Ethnic
and territorial minorities or suppressed classes question the dominating group's right to rule over them, and neighboring governments covet territories and resources. The ability of a government
to withstand pressures from within or without depends on its
ability to maintain a stance of potential violence. It may be a
benevolent regime — its arts and commerce may flourish — but
its continued existence depends absolutely on its capacity to
destroy peace in order to maintain it. Few governments are able
to maintain this stance for more than a few generations. The nearly
constant warfare between territories, dynasties, classes, and nations
(to which students of history soon become accustomed) is the

dance of sovereignty as it flows between communities. Each war, each organized act of violence, is a shifting psychic boundary between one sovereign entity and another. Remarkable degrees of strength and stability have been maintained through the centuries by dominating classes or families, but the tendency over time is toward internal disintegration or external absorption. All governments die in time.

Disintegration from within reduces the scale of sovereign units while absorption from without increases it. Large governments tend to break up into smaller units, and small governments tend to be taken over by larger neighboring units. These tendencies balance against one another, but through history the balance has been tipped slightly toward larger-scale government. Amid the chaos of warring sovereignties, their average size has increased with time. Clans become tribes; tribes become confederations. Neolithic villages of prehistoric times give way to the city–states of ancient times, which are in turn absorbed by great empires. The fiefdoms of the Middle Ages slowly and painfully merge into nation–states. Governments continue both to disintegrate from within and to expand from without, but the equilibrium between the two is tilted toward expansion.

Many reasons can be given for this. Economic growth requires a broader territorial resource base and greater economic interdependence. Increased trade across borders diminishes the meaning of the borders themselves. Improvements in transportation and communication lead to wider knowledge of distant areas and greater psychological identity among distant peoples. But each of these is more an effect than a cause of broadened sovereignty; there is no specialization and interdependence without civil order and no trade without political stability. Transportation and communication do not exist without protection. Each of these takes place only within the context of established sovereignty. The arts of peace exist by virtue of the arts of war; it is through advances in the arts of war that the general scale of political sovereignty has increased over time. It is through better weapons that we have higher levels of civilization. Bronze, for instance, is better than stone or wood for cutting human flesh. Those who have bronze weapons can kill or threaten to kill more people than those who do not. Larger territories can be controlled because those who oppose central authority can be eliminated more efficiently. Larger territories in turn facilitated control of copper and tin supplies (the elements from which bronze is made). Bronze can be used for tools, jewelry, and works of art as well as for weaponry, but its military application comes first. It is bronze weaponry that built the ancient city–states of Egypt, Syria, and Mesopotamia at the expense of independent neolithic villages.

An improvement over bronze is iron. Harder, stronger, and less brittle, iron weapons are to bronze what bronze is to stone or wood. One of the most important applications of iron was defensive weaponry. Iron shields could withstand the impact of enemy swords and missiles, especially if used in formation. The development during the early Iron Age of the Greek phalanx gave great advantage to those with the discipline to stand and fight as an organized unit. A solid block of well-trained troops standing shoulder to shoulder and shield to shield wielding only short jabbing weapons could defeat a much larger force of scattered individuals, no matter how ferocious their offensive capabilities. The Romans adopted and improved on the Greek phalanx, stressing order, training, and discipline over individual prowess, and later in the Iron Age, the Romans were able to weld the entire Western world into a single sovereign entity.

After the disintegration of the Roman Empire in late antiquity, the Western world remained divided into fragments of local and regional government for more than a thousand years. Government existed from time to time on something like the national level but sovereignty did not. Vassals were able to maintain their independence from kings with the use of stone fortification and iron-plated armor. A king was not a true sovereign, only a first among equals;

with superior numbers he could defeat a vassal or two in open battle, but he could not defeat all of them at the same time. He had no strategic or technological advantage over them. A vassal could retreat to his castle and force the king to risk a costly frontal assault or a prolonged and expensive siege. The creation of national sovereignty was brought to bear by the king in time but only with the introduction of gunpowder in the early modern period.

The earliest and most important use of gunpowder was not in handheld weaponry, but in artillery, on both land and sea. (Manual weaponry was already revolutionized by the English longbow, which was able to send a missile through the armor plating of medieval cavalry. At the Battle of Crecy in 1346, ten thousand English commoners wiped out about twice as many French noblemen on horseback.) Artillery favored centralized government because it made local defense nearly impossible. Where a medieval vassal could defy his king by hiding behind a stone wall, an early modern vassal soon found himself standing in a pile of rubble. Only the king, with greater financial and manpower resources, could afford to buy artillery pieces and pay full-time professionals to employ them effectively. At sea, only the king could afford a modern navy equipped with cannon. Sovereignty on the scale of the modern nation–state was a direct result of a gunpowder-based military technology.

Sovereignty might well have remained on the level of the nation–state had military technology remained stagnant in the current era. But the development of intercontinental weaponry has made national defense as impractical now as local defense was four hundred years ago. Nuclear weapons are entirely offensive; there is no way to use them defensively and no way to defend against them effectively. We may like to think of them as defending the nation, but they can "defend" only by offending the enemy in the worst way. The enemy, in turn, cannot truly defend himself without utterly annihilating us. Modern weapons nullify natural defenses as well. The greatest defenses many nations have had are mountain ranges, oceans, rivers, and sheer distance from potential enemies, but these mean nothing in an age of intercontinental ballistic missiles. America, in particular, has enjoyed the protection of huge oceans on either side but now finds herself liable to multimegaton attack from the sky at any moment with only a few minute's warning. We are suddenly much closer to those who may do us harm. It is true that a degree of defense may be achieved at some time in the future by intercepting a portion of incoming ballistic missiles, but it will always be easier and cheaper for the enemy to make bigger, smarter, and more numerous missiles. Very few need get through.

At present, only a few nations have nuclear weapons. Fewer have the ability to deliver them on intercontinental or medium-range missiles. But nuclear weapons will be everywhere in the coming years. Like every other major technological development, they will be sought by nations large and small, as well as by insurgencies, terrorist cults, and independence movements within nations. Existing nuclear powers will attempt to control nuclear "proliferation" as long as possible, but the cat is already out of the bag. Within a few decades, nuclear bombs and delivery systems will be generally available in all parts of the world. As long as there is no global authority to control them, they will not be illegal, and as long as a nation has the right to defend itself, having nuclear weaponry will not be immoral.

The eventual absorption of national by supranational sovereignty is a technological imperative. It will happen because there is no way, short of annihilation, that it cannot happen. The scale of political sovereignty must expand with the power of nuclear technology, and there is very little room for it to expand below the global level. We will have global sovereignty whether or not we choose it: There is no longer enough territory on the planet to divide among independent sovereignties. No portion of the earth's surface is now defensible in any realistic sense against any other portion. The nation will survive — but not as a sovereign territorial entity.

But how is it that this will come about? How will humanity suddenly become more important than nationality? We have already noted that most people will risk death before allowing sovereignty to flow from existing relations: How, then, will they ever allow sovereignty to move from the national to the global level? I believe the answer is quite simple: They *will* risk death. They are risking it now. The horrible potential of nuclear weaponry is so great and so generally feared that the psychic bonds of naïve nationalism have already begun to melt. Many people already know that the nation will have to give way to the world. The more delicate question becomes, Is an abstract awareness of nuclear potential enough? Or must people see actual nuclear war before they allow sovereignty to flow? How close to the real thing do we have to get before we feel it moving through our minds and bodies? How tangible must the fear become? The answer to this question is, I fear, equally simple: Everyone knows what nuclear weapons can do, but there are other things to think about. We do not yet feel the wholeness in our hearts that would make the weapons superfluous, and we will not feel it until after we have looked death in the face.

Sovereignty is not created by design; it is a matter of subconsciousness and not of logic. However, underlying patterns of political relations can be identified and manipulated by the conscious mind at critical moments. We *can* design the particular forms they take. When we are looking death in the face, we will divert the flow of sovereignty in one direction or another, depending on who we think we are. We should prepare for that moment. Until then, be it known that anyone contemplating sovereign relations that do not yet exist must stand before the potential violence enfolded in those that do.

3. The Nation–State

When Cenwealh was dead (that is 672 A.D.) during whose reign Leuthere had been made bishop, subkings took upon themselves the government of the kingdom (regnum), dividing it up and ruling for about ten years. While they were reigning, Leuthere died and was succeeded by Haedde, who had been consecrated in London by Theodore. During his episcopate the subkings were conquered and removed and Caedwalla assumed the overlordship.[1]
— *The Venerable Bede on West Saxon subkings*

WE DO NOT SHARE A POLITICAL PARADIGM WITH MEDIEVAL Europe. The sovereign nation–state, for us the basic unit of human organization and around which all other types of organization are built, did not exist five or six hundred years ago. France, England, Italy, Spain, Germany, and Russia, the building blocks of modern European history, were at the time more geographic than political expressions.

This makes it difficult for us to grasp life as it was during the Middle Ages. Too often we look back at what was happening in ninth-century Burgundy or Wessex in terms of what has happened since. We think of the accomplishments of Alfred the Great and Charlemagne as early attempts at "nation building" only because the general areas in which they operated later became nation–states. We point to people like Henry II of England and Philip Augustus of France because what they did fits into a pattern that has since become visible. They were early examples of what we are now. Had some other political form succeeded — say, the medieval ideal of a cosmopolitan Christian empire — we would pay more attention to popes and Holy Roman emperors. We would be looking at Charlemagne and Henry II through an entirely different perspective, emphasizing the transnational dimensions of their empires instead of trends toward national consolidation that took place within separate parts of their empires.

The nation–state is a coincidence of government, language, and geography. In its idealized state, it is a single sovereign governmental entity embodying a particular type of people, or nation, speaking a single language within a specific and well-defined physical region. There are no such perfect nation–states, of course, but the ideal is strong and very real in the minds of all modern peoples. It is without question the accepted paradigm of modern civilized life. We no longer hear of people striving to build tribes or empires or city–states; we hear of people building and living for nations. Tribes and empires and city–states remain, but they are exceptions to the rule or are considered stages through which peoples must pass in the inevitable march toward nationhood. Look at a map of the world today and you will see a world of nation–states.

Look at a map of ancient times and you will see a world of tribes and empires and city–states. For the ancient Greeks the city–state, or *polis*, was the ideal form of government, and constituted civilization itself. The English words *polite, political, police,* and *policy* convey this sense of civilized living. When Aristotle said that man is a *political* animal he meant quite literally that the difference between man and animal is that man lives in the polis. The polis was the great success and the great failure of Greek civilization; Athens, Corinth, Sparta, Chalcis, Eretria, Megara, and Thebes were all independently sovereign city–states. Each possessed its own particular genius and each its own army and system of defense. Wars among them were never-ending. A generation would rarely pass without bitter violence between neighboring city–states. The ancient Greeks all spoke a common language, occupied a distinct geography, and considered themselves the same people, but they never developed a national government. Each Greek was a Spartan or Athenian first and a Greek second. After the destruction of Athens and the exhaustion of Sparta in the Peloponnesian War, the Greeks were no longer able to defend themselves from the non-Greek world and soon lost their independence to the Macedonians and later to the Romans.

The ancient empire was an outgrowth of the city–state. Usually originating at a single capital city — whether Rome, Ur, Athens, Babylon, or Nineveh — the ancient empire rarely limited itself to a particular geography or nationality, incorporating within its sovereign reach any number and variety of territories, peoples, and languages. There was no attempt to match sovereignty with nationality. A dominant nationality would rule wherever and whomever happened to be conquered by its armies.

An invention that greatly facilitated the growth of empires was written language. Large territorial expanses could be governed effectively only through the keeping of written records and the delivery of written messages over long distances. But hieroglyphics and cuneiform, the first written languages, were not based on phonetic alphabets and therefore not specific to spoken languages. People of different nationalities, who could not communicate through spoken language, all used the same written language. Written language was an indispensable tool of imperial control but not the vehicle of national culture that it has become in the modern world.

The nation–state was not the political paradigm of the ancient world, and very few nationalities were able to maintain territorial integrity and political independence in the face of imperial power. An exception to this was the ancient Hebrew kingdom of David and Solomon. For about seventy years after the decline of the neighboring Hittite and Egyptian empires and before it disintegrated from within, the Hebrew nation maintained both political independence and territorial integrity. Had it not split into the northern Kingdom of Israel and the southern Kingdom of Judea, it might have gone on to form its own empire. But the sovereignty of the Hebrew state was not as integral to the Hebrew nation as it would be to a modern nation. The Hebrews and their Judean and Israeli descendants defined themselves less by government than by religion. Their religion was one of nationality, and their God a god of nationality. For this reason, they have survived into modern times as a nation if not as a nation–state. They retain to this day a strong national identity even though they did not enjoy national sovereignty for more than two thousand years. The northern kingdom fell to the Assyrian empire in 722 B.C. and the southern kingdom to the Chaldeans in 528 B.C. They reestablished themselves as the independent nation–state of Israel in the twentieth century. But the enduring legacy of the Hebrew people is its close association of God and nationality even to the present day.

In the Near East, India, and China, empires remained the prevailing political paradigm until recent times. In Europe, for a thousand years after the decline of Rome, the ideal state remained a united Christian Empire modeled after the old Roman Empire, though this was never achieved. Remnants of declining Roman provincial culture merged with invading Germanic tribal cultures to produce a long period of manorial feudalism that was neither imperial nor national. Two factors that led to the formation of European nation–states in the early modern period were the decline of Latin as the universal language of religion and literature and the invention of the printing press.

The printed word was the first mass medium. It defined and unified emerging national languages and strengthened the formation of separate national identities. Before 1500, regional dialects varied so greatly within a single nation as to be mutually unintelligible, and there were no clear distinctions between what constituted a language and what constituted a dialect. A traveler from

Warwick could barely understand what was said in Cornwall, and an Alsatian might have better luck with his French-speaking neighbor down the road than with another German in Bavaria. But as uniform national literary traditions arose, they promoted uniform spoken languages and provided people with a means to identify with fellow citizens from one end of the country to another.

Nationalism is most simply defined as the primary identification of individual people with their linguistic group. It was not a major force in medieval times in Europe or anywhere else because there was no sense of just what a nation might be. There was no clear territorial boundary between one language and another and no clear correspondence between language and political sovereignty. There were great differences between the ways people spoke in London, Cologne, and Marseille, but there were no national languages for England, Germany, or France. Language was a local affair. One could generally communicate with people in the next town or village but only with difficulty in the next shire or province. It was impossible to say where "French" began and "German" left off. To this day, rural people in the border areas of Alsace and Lorraine think of themselves as French but speak a dialect of German. Political power was also a mostly local affair, with only weak, indirect ties to a king at a more-or-less national level. Enemies could as easily be found in the next manor or borough as across the Rhine or the Pyrenees. People identified with their town or village and with Christian Europe as a whole more than with any one nation. Their "country" was what they could see on a clear day.

The rise of the nation–state in modern times is related to two distinct technological developments: the printing press and gunpowder. The printing press promoted the growth and standardization of national languages at the expense of Latin and of local spoken dialects; gunpowder promoted the growth of larger units of sovereign power roughly corresponding to the new linguistic groups.

The effect of the printing press is best shown by William Caxton (1422–1491), an early English printer, translator, and observer of his times. Caxton describes the diversity of the English language through time and place and the problem of choosing between local usages in his translations:

> certaynly our langage now vsed varyeth ferre from that whiche was vsed and spoken when I was borne.... And the comyn englysshe that is spoken in one shyre varyeth from another.

He illustrates this with a story of how a merchant from another part of England

> cam into an hows and axed for mete; and specyally he axyed after eggys; and the goode wyf answerde that she coude speke no frenshe. And the merchaunt was angry, for he also coude speke no frenshe.... And theene at laste another sayd that he wolde haue "eyren" then the good wyf sayd that she vnderstod hym wel. Loo, what sholde a man in thyse dayes now wryte, "egges" or "eyren"?

Caxton, of course, had no dictionary. He also found himself forced to choose between the coarse everyday language of the laborer and that of the "gentylman":

> therefor in a meane bytwene bothe I haue reduced and translated this sayd booke in to our englysshe, not ouer rude ne curyous, but in suche termes as shall be vnderstanden, by goddys grace, accordynge to my copye. [2]

While he was busy pondering usages, Caxton printed more than a hundred new books in standardized English and distributed them throughout the land. Others were busy at the same time with printing machines in Germany, Italy, and France.

Individual people within each country, though living at considerable distances from one another, were soon reading the same books in the exact same language. As literary education spread, so too did a common national usage in oral as well as written language. People in various parts of a country identified with one another as being the "same" type of people, as opposed to those who spoke or wrote in some distinctly "other" language. Thus were born nationalities but not nation–states. Nation–states were created only with an expanded scope of sovereign power that paralleled the substitution of explosive for manual weaponry.

But what is the connection between language and sovereignty? Why do nationalities turn into nation–states? They do not automatically: Kurds, Basques, and Palestinians do not have national independence to this day. Until the last few decades, sovereign empires in Eastern Europe encompassed several major linguistic groups. Language and sovereignty seem to connect best when they coincide with a geographic setting that is favorable in scale, definition, and natural defense. To become a sovereign community, a modern linguistic group must occupy a territory that is defensible with gunpowder-based military technology. Too small a group on too small a territory is likely to be swallowed by its neighbors, and too large a group on too ill-defined a territory is likely to remain decentralized. Nationalities that become successful nation–states must also occupy territories with properly placed mountains ranges, rivers, deserts, and oceans. They must have territories that are easily defended but, more important, easily defined. It is of utmost importance that they know who they are in contrast to who they are not. Political and linguistic lines converge best where they both coincide with clear geographic lines.

England, an island nation with the most highly defined geography, was the first European nation to be unified into a sovereign state. Like other areas of Europe, England was divided in the early Middle Ages into an array of petty kingdoms and subkingdoms, all in a state of internecine warfare. But being relatively small, a centralized kingdom was more readily established there than was possible on the Continent. By the late Middle Ages, most of the island had become politically and linguistically consolidated. Celtic minorities remained but did not threaten national existence. The North Sea and the English Channel provided the English king with a natural line of defense against attacking Danes and Vikings and also provided a barrier to his own imperial ambitions on the Continent. The Welsh to the west were subdued and incorporated into the kingdom, and the Irish were safely across the water. The only real terrestrial frontier was to the north, where the Scots periodically invaded — and were invaded by — the English. To the east, south, and west, the seas provided a clear definition of where England began and where it ended: There was no gradual thinning out of English language and sovereign authority. The seas provided sufficient natural defense for Henry VIII, in the sixteenth century, to avoid the expense of a full-time standing army. But they also provided a limit within which England could confine and concentrate her energies. After repeated attempts in the later Middle Ages to seize and hold territories in France, the English soon gave up and turned inward to build and consolidate the nation from within. Their failure to maintain sovereignty in France heightened their self-identity as an island nation and allowed for a corresponding consolidation of national identity among the French.

Spain — with nearly equally favorable geography — consolidated soon thereafter. France was slower to consolidate, with less geographic definition and more room than England for competing powers to arise from within. Still, with the Atlantic to the west and north, the Rhine and Alps to the east, and the Mediterranean and Pyrenees to the south, France was gifted geographically compared to other European countries. Often at war with the English and Spanish, France had clear geographic boundaries with these countries: They did not threaten her identity as a separate nation. More troublesome were frontier borders to the southeast with

Italy and to the north and east with Holland, Belgium, and Germany. Borders have shifted back and forth in these areas, depending on who has won the last war, and national and linguistic identities in border areas are less defined than in central provinces.

East of France, the lack of geographic features has slowed the development of nationalism. Poland and Germany, with very little geographic definition, did not become nation–states until the eighteenth and nineteenth centuries, and Ukraine and Belarus, with none at all, only became nation–states at the end of the twentieth century. Russia suffered from foreign invasion and lack of distinct national identity with its vast open plains to the east, west, and south. The only nation with good geographic definition that failed to consolidate in the early modern period is Italy. This is explicable in terms of the persistence, particularly in the north, of the ancient paradigm of the city–state.

Despite its more varied geography, the concept of nationalism reached southeastern Europe only at the turn of the twentieth century. As the Ottoman Empire declined, Serbs, Slovenes, Croats, Romanians, Bulgarians, Greeks, Macedonians, Montenegrins, Bosnians, and Albanians all strove for independence from the Turks and from each other. But linguistic and territorial distinctions were unclear. Enclaves of Serbs lived in Bosnia and Croatia, while enclaves of Croats, Albanians, and Macedonians occupied parts of Serbia. Croats, Serbs, and Bosnians all speak the same language: Their cultural distinctiveness is more a matter of religion and custom than of nationality in the Western European sense. In fact, the nation–state seems to be a purely Western European concept artificially and inappropriately imposed on the Balkan Mountains.

The concept of the nation–state as a predominant political form arose in the fifteenth and sixteenth centuries in Western Europe with a convergence of technological and geographic factors. It later spread to Central and Eastern Europe, where geographic definition is less apparent or missing altogether. Language alone is now sufficient to define nationality in Europe. But the concept of "nation" has transcended even its linguistic definition in other parts of the world. The farther we go from Europe, the more artificial the nation–state becomes — and the less appropriate. In Africa, Asia, and South America, independent "nations" have arisen without respect to linguistic distinction. Rather than incorporating a distinct people with a distinct language, history, and geography, nation–states in these parts of the world are mostly former colonies. Where one nation ends and another begins is often the same place one colonial department ended and another began. The boundary between Bolivia and Peru cuts the Aymara and Chechua nations virtually in half. The urban areas of both countries are dominated by the same Spanish-speaking intelligencia. In Africa, the Somali *nation* does not include Somali peoples living in Ethiopia, Kenya, and Djibouti but does include a number of Arab minorities. In Asia, the Kurdish people are divided by borders separating Iraq, Turkey, and Iran. By the European ideal of the nation–state, the entire area that we call the Middle East — from Morocco across North Africa to Egypt and on through the Saudi peninsula and Mesopotamia — should be a single independent nation. Instead, artificial divisions have been imposed and given the designation of nationality. The European concept of the nation–state was projected onto former colonial dependencies without regard to actual nationality. The result has been political unrest among minorities in former colonies, unrest that will continue until actual nations become nation–states or the paradigm is abandoned.

The places nationalism has been most disastrous for the peoples it is supposed to consolidate are where there are no clear geographic lines to correspond with linguistic lines. Where diverse ethnic groups occupy the same territory or where minorities form enclaves within larger national communities, territorial defense becomes a physical impossibility and national sovereignty seems an unrealistic dream (for instance, the Balkans of southern Europe, the Sudetenland of the former Czechoslovakia, and the Azeri and Armenian enclaves of the Nagorno–Karabakh region). Peoples in these areas become highly conscious of national differences but find themselves with no practical means of establishing separate sovereignties. The result is constant ethnic tension that periodically breaks into open warfare.

As we watch the map of modern Europe take shape through the centuries, we are comforted to see the fulfillment of what we consider a fixed and inevitable paradigm. Each nation develops a clearly defined territory with its own distinct color. But as the nation–state paradigm moves to other parts of the world, the two technologies that make it possible — printing and gunpowder — are becoming obsolete. They are, in fact, obsolete already. The print medium, which has served to standardize and solidify linguistic identity over extended territories, is giving way to an electronic video technology whose visual messages transcend linguistic distinction. People know what is going on in the world outside of their nation–state and can access and *see* it instantaneously without translation. As more people watch the same things, they develop common experience, and with common experience comes identity. Racial, linguistic, and cultural differences remain, but the emotional underpinnings of nationalism are eroding rapidly. People continue to identify with their linguistic group but are beginning to question nationality as a primary political allegiance when it conflicts with a more broad-based human identity.

As video overtakes the predominance of print media, nuclear weapons technology overtakes the predominance of gunpowder-based weaponry. Like the early modern artillery that preceded it, nuclear weaponry is primarily offensive in effect; it favors the centralized expansion of political power at the expense of local defense. As a result, the territorial expanse of sovereign political communities will grow very rapidly in the near future to a scale much larger than that of linguistic groups — at least as large, in fact, as the entire earth. There will be no territory of the planet defensible against any other territory, and no geographic basis for sovereign stability on anything smaller than the global level. The territorial expanse of any future sovereign community will be that of the earth itself. There are no castle walls thick enough or tall enough to withstand intercontinental war in the twenty-first century.

Without national sovereignty, what will happen to national languages, customs, and cultures? Does global unity mean the end of diversity? There is no doubt that local traditions are diminished by international travel, business, and media and that the loss of national sovereignty will in some ways further erode the protection of national culture from global influence. In a nation–state, the individual's primary identity is with the nation; he is a nationality first and a human being after that. He defines himself as innately separate and distinct from people in other nations, and this identity helps preserve the integrity of his language, dress, and aspects of his political beliefs and religious expression. Global sovereignty will mean a loss of this primary identity: He will become a human being first and a nationality second. But does this mean the *loss* of nationality?

The challenge under global unity will be to preserve nationality even as national sovereignty is lost. Political and economic mechanisms will have to be created that encourage human diversity within the context of political unity. This will in time become a better way to preserve diversity than nationalism itself. Now, without global unity, indigenous cultures are already dying out. Chinese, American, and European products are already finding their way across the plains of central Asia and up the river valleys of southern Africa. English is spoken, written, and sung everywhere. Japanese cartoons are pervasive in Central America. The same soft drinks are advertised and consumed in Paris, Bangkok, and Ouagadougou. The loss of local production, local custom, and local self-reliance is happening without global unity — positive evidence that unity cannot be its cause. Global unity may, ironically, prove to be a means of restoring national identity in some cases. When diversity is no longer imposed by force of arms, it may be protected and encouraged by legislation specially designed for the purpose.

The world should, for example, learn to protect and encourage local agriculture. Culture is closely integrated with the production and trade of food products, and diversity is strongest and most pronounced in rural areas. It will be best protected by protecting local economies from undue exposure to world food markets. Every culture interacts with the particularities of its natural habitat in the finding, growing, hunting, cooking, storing, and marketing of what it eats. Cultural diversity is based on biodiversity; the richness in variety of human life is a reflection of the living wealth of the earth herself, from the rain forests of West Africa to the plains of North America to the Siberian arctic. This is where diversity begins, and where it is most under attack. Local agriculture is being destroyed by free trade agreements that subject small-scale production to open competition with global agribusiness. The hoes and water buffalo of Southeast Asia are forced to compete with the combines and agrichemicals of Kansas and Saskatchewan. This produces cheaper food in the short run, but it also destroys the economic base of local culture and creates dependency. Food becomes available only when hard currency is available and only when producing countries have surpluses. Emergencies in banking, commerce, and transportation in far-off places can lead to starvation at home.

Locally based agriculture is also the most likely to be humane and environmentally friendly. The scale of production required by international agribusiness promotes the overuse of chemical fertilizers and pesticides, monoculture, concentration of animals in large feedlots and poultry factories, waste concentrations, and pollution. Production on smaller scales favors crop diversity, use of wastes for fertilizer, free-range animal husbandry, and a knowledge within local populations of where food comes from and how its production affects the environment. This can be preserved in a world economy with trade legislation that factors cultural diversity and the environment into commodity prices. Import tariffs should be allowed for some crops in some areas, and it should be coordinated on the global level and not on the national level. Free trade should be encouraged on the world market where appropriate, but it would be inappropriate if it were allowed to destroy local communities. A well-balanced global economy will utilize market forces to spur competition where it serves human needs but must trust human intervention where it does not.

A global culture is emerging in and around national societies, but it need not be bland and featureless and need not threaten indigenous culture. It cannot be stopped; it can only be creatively diverted. The more conscious the process of globalization, the more diversity may be preserved. Cultures will be lost and absorbed, indigenous peoples will die out, and a certain homogenous quality will arise in international life no matter what we do. But this process will not result in the sterile monoculture that many fear. There will always be diversity in language, custom, religion, and outlook — a diversity that can be encouraged and augmented with good government. Separate cultural traditions will remain even as a single political identity is formed. Differences may at some point become less geographically based and less dependent on accidents of birth and upbringing, but they will endure as long as human nature is allowed to roam where it will.

The sovereign nation–state is a recent concept, historically speaking, and only one of many models of human political organization. Humanity can survive without it. We need to realize this to make it true. We will not survive with it.

4. The Trend toward Global Unity

A General association of nations must be formed under specific covenants for the purpose of affording mutual guarantees of political independence and territorial integrity to great and small states alike.

— *Woodrow Wilson's fourteenth point*

WAR HAS GOTTEN A BAD NAME IN MODERN TIMES. TRENches, poison gas, machine guns, and neutron bombs have taken much of the manhood out of dying for one's country, and there is a distinct trend now toward resolving disputes between nations without violence. But it is a weak trend, overshadowed by the many conflicts it is supposed to prevent. Its history is a sad story of impotence and failure, with but few shining moments of success.

Internationalism — or the belief that nations can and should prevent war through negotiating differences in a systematic manner — can be traced back at least as far as the early nineteenth century.[3] In 1815, after twenty-five years of the worst warfare in history (beginning with the French Revolution and ending with the defeat of Napoleon at Waterloo), there was a consensus among the major powers of Europe that something ought to be done to prevent it from happening again. A loosely organized system of congresses evolved beginning with the peace settlement itself, the Congress of Vienna, and continuing intermittently through 1822 at Aix-la-Chapelle, Troppau, Laibach, and Verona. The great champion of peace was Czar Alexander I of Russia, whose Holy Alliance established a set of divinely ordained principles by which all European powers, great and small, were to guide their relations with their subjects and with each other. The peace was to be enforced by the Quadruple Alliance, consisting of Britain, Austria, Prussia, and Russia, which was the old alliance that had developed during the war. France was allowed to join in 1818, and it became the Quintuple Alliance. It was supposed to band together whenever there was a threat to the general peace and to act in concert against whatever nation, revolution, or upheaval disturbed the status quo.

The military power of a united Europe was a formidable force, certainly sufficient to put down any attempts to rock the boat. But its unity depended entirely on the goodwill in which it was conceived. There was no continuing organization between congresses, no permanent council, and no systematic means by which offenses could be adjudicated. Members were supposed to meet as offenses arose and to respond to the call to arms without hesitation, voluntarily coordinating their efforts as they had in the alliance against Napoleon. There was no question that the five members were themselves above reproach; they could not possibly disturb the new order because they *were* the new order. Consequently, there was not the slightest mention of limiting the absolute sovereignty of member nations. Each could do as it pleased; it was assumed that coordinated activity on the international level would be spontaneous and mutually beneficial and that there would be no need for supranational direction. No *one* would rule another; they were all friends, after all, and equals.

The congress system with the Quintuple Alliance failed almost before it started because it assumed that nothing would ever change. The Big Five would always stay the same Big Five, there would be no more revolutions or independence movements, and military technology would remain limited to muskets, cannon, and sailcloth. Not only did it refuse to recognize the future, it actively emulated the past. It was distinctly *reactionary*. The wars of the last quarter century had been the fault of commoners — people like Napoleon and his followers, who tried to overthrow the natural aristocracy. Stability could be maintained only through "legitimate" rulers — people who had been born to their positions in society. All others would have to be deposed. The Alliance stood against everything the modern world has become. How, then, can we construe so backward a movement as being the beginning of a trend for the future?

The Quintuple Alliance took place at a moment of international cooperation in which the horrors of war were fresh. It was significant not for what it attempted (much less for what it did) but for its ideal of enforced international peace. It was the first time that modern nation–states worked together not against a particular war but against war itself. It was supposed to be not a temporary agreement or a conditional alliance against a common enemy but a permanent working order that would make the whole world a better place for people. The ideal of world peace was for the first time tried out in the real world.

It was not to be tried again for a hundred years. The League of Nations, like the congress system, was conceived after the horrors of a major world war. Everyone agreed that the world could not stand another such war and that some permanent structure of peace should be created. Ten million people had just died in World War I — the most ghastly and destructive conflict in history. A whole generation of British, French, Russians, Germans, Austrians, and Italians was lost and nothing was won. No nation came out better than it had gone in (with the exception of the United States). All that had been accomplished after four years of man-made hell was mutual destruction and exhaustion. The League of Nations, proposed by President Woodrow Wilson and eagerly accepted by a war-weary Europe, promised that it would never happen again.

The League was an great improvement over the congress system. It was established with a permanent secretariat and headquarters and governed by a General Assembly of all member nations and a Council of the great powers. League members were guaranteed protection against aggression but were obliged to submit all disputes or claims to arbitration and to abstain from war for at least three months after any potential award. There were to be no secret meetings or agreements between nations; all treaties were to be public and registered with the League. In addition to its role as peacekeeper, the League was to devote itself to problems in the fields of health, disarmament, and labor conditions.

But like the congresses of the early 1800s, the League was never a global organization. Argentina, one of its few non-European members, introduced a measure in 1921 to admit all sovereign nations in the world, but the measure was rejected. Germany and Austria were not admitted initially because they had lost the war; Russia was not admitted until 1934 for ideological reasons; and the United States, which had proposed the League, refused to join because it might infringe on national sovereignty. Member nations could also pull out of the League whenever it proved inconvenient to their purposes. Argentina pulled out after its measure was turned down, Japan pulled out in order to attack China, and Germany pulled out in order to begin the next world war.

Like the congress system before it, the League never attempted to limit in any way the sovereign power of its member nations despite American fears that it would. In fact, the League was specifically created "for the purpose of affording mutual guarantees of political independence and territorial integrity" of its members — that is, to *preserve* national sovereignty. Nations were not supposed to go to war in any aggressive way, but they retained (with League sanction) the right to "self-defense" and, by inference, the right to define it. Hitler always claimed, as his tanks rolled across the border in September of 1939, that he was defending the Fatherland against "Polish aggression."

The League of Nations was a significant organizational advance over the congress system, but it failed because it depended on its members to enforce measures against themselves. There was, in fact, very little substance to the League other than its members. It existed for their convenience and at their convenience.

A small step forward was taken after the far greater destruction of World War II. After the war, the United Nations — originally formed as an alliance among Great Britain, the Soviet Union, and the United States against the Axis powers — assumed the peacekeeping role of the League of Nations. There were some differences, the primary difference being that the U.N. *is* a truly global body, at least in scope. There are more than 190 members from all parts of the globe, each with a vote in the General Assembly. But the real power of the U.N., to the extent that there is any real power, is with the Security Council, controlled by five permanent members: the United States, Russia, Great Britain, France, and China. These five can impose their will on smaller nations but never on each other, as each retains a veto power over any measure taken. The United Nations has been effective many times in resolving international differences and in sending armed "peacekeepers" to trouble spots, mostly in Africa and the Middle East where there is no clear domination by a permanent Security Council member. But the U.N. can never perform its most important mission, which is to prevent general war from breaking out between major military powers.

The fundamental problem with the United Nations is the same as that with its predecessor: It has no real power. As long as the major powers are in a mood to cooperate — as they were immediately after World War II and only on occasion since then — the U.N. can be effective, but when the major powers oppose each other as they did during the Cold War, it is impotent. The U.N. cannot prevent nuclear war from taking effect because the nuclear powers can prevent the U.N. from taking effect. It in no way limits national powers; it merely coordinates the powers of separate nations. Its membership is global, but it is not a global *power*; its structure is international but not supranational.

The United Nations is evolving rapidly despite its structural weakness and lack of political and military power. There is a greater demand now than ever before for international order. When famine strikes or war breaks out, there is an expectation throughout the world that "somebody" ought to do something about it, and the U.N. is the obvious choice. With the end of the Cold War, the U.N. can operate without provoking superpower vetoes and can intervene at times in the internal affairs of smaller nations. With a more neutral international climate in which to work, it can undertake or authorize international missions, humanitarian or punitive, without threatening the position of any one superpower. It is not the role of the U.N. that has changed so much as the scope of its operations. It has been actively involved in keeping peace in El Salvador, Namibia, Mozambique, Western Sahara, Angola, Cambodia, South West Africa, Somalia, Iraq, Bosnia, Mozambique, Israel, Lebanon, and the former Yugoslavia, among other places. It is in the news; we hear of it more than we used to. There seems to be a growing expectation that it *ought* to be the one taking care of world problems and that it ought to be doing more than it is doing. But without political and military power, adequate and reliable funding, *and* a clear mandate for more than nominal intervention, the U.N. can accomplish very little of what is expected of it.

The huge new demand for global order in the absence of an effective U.N. has led to an interesting new role for NATO — the North Atlantic Treaty Organization. NATO is, of course, anything but a global organization. Conceived in the early years of the Cold War, its purpose was to prepare for and to fight the next world war. It has succeeded in keeping the peace in Europe the old-fashioned way — by preparing for war. Its mission is exclusively military, and its membership is limited to the enemies (or former enemies) of the Soviet Union and its Warsaw Pact allies. Its identity, therefore, has depended on its enemy; without the enemy, NATO no longer knows what it is supposed to be. Its use in Bosnia in the 1990s is an experiment in a new way of keeping peace — that is, by enforcing an international order. But it has no legitimate political presence in Bosnia; NATO is there only because it has the firepower to do the job — the firepower the U.N. does not have. Without legitimate global sovereignty, its firepower will not be able to keep the peace for long. The people will tolerate being policed by others only as long as the horrors of the recent war remain fresh.

But the NATO mission in Bosnia is of great historical importance. Thousands of soldiers from many nations, including the major powers, went off to peace instead of to war. This was a realistic attempt to undo a war, and it indicates that human civilization is evolving toward a global order. We will learn from the NATO mission, and much of what we do about wars in the future will be based the outcome in Bosnia. NATO may be called on for similar missions in the future and will then have to develop an entirely new identity. In fact, it will no longer be itself. NATO may become a transitional stage between the perceived need for a stable international order and a permanent institutional means of creating it. Eventually, the job NATO has been called to do must be done by an organization representing the will of the world's peoples.

From 1990 to 2003, U.N. interests often coincided with those of the United States. With the decline of Soviet power, the United States involved itself militarily in the Persian Gulf, Somalia, and Haiti — all under U.N. auspices. With the exception of Haiti, these interventions could not have taken place before the end of the Cold War. The U.S. in each case took on the role of enforcer of international law, responding to the demand for international order without ostensible ulterior motive and, often, successfully.

Even the U.S.-led invasion of Iraq in 1991 was undertaken with a clear mandate from the U.N. to counter Iraqi aggression against Kuwait. These actions can be interpreted as an altruistic American response to global needs or as the U.S. using the U.N. to further its own national interests. Both interpretations are true, and we need not choose between them; what we saw in this period was the convergence, however temporary, of American interests with international interests.

But the world cannot depend on national power to uphold international order. When U.S. interests diverged from those of the U.N. 2003, international order dissolved into international war. The American administration, expecting the United Nations to follow rather than lead, accused it of "doing nothing" about Iraq's supposed stockpile of chemical, biological, and possibly nuclear weapons, even though U.N. inspectors were in Iraq at the time, busily trying to locate them. Convinced that the Iraqis were dodging inept U.N. inspectors and hiding weapons that the American president and his advisers "knew they had," the United States invaded Iraq without provocation, overthrew its government, and began its own weapons inspection program. In January 2004, after seven months on the job, the chief American weapons inspector resigned, having found no such weapons and suggesting that they may have been destroyed in the 1990s while Iraq was undergoing U.N. inspections.

The U.N. should have prevented the 2003 Iraq War. It should have had the power to stand up to American bullying in the Security Council, and it should have had the authority to prevent the U.S. from going to war without a resolution. If the U.N. had decided that the Iraqi administration was a threat to international peace, it should have had the resources to intervene on its own. Only a world body representing the interests of all people everywhere has the legitimacy to intervene in the internal affairs of any nation, especially if that intervention involves regime change. The Bush administration had as much right to attack Baghdad and

overthrow Saddam Hussein as Hussein had to attack
Washington D.C. and overthrow Bush.

The development of weapons of mass destruction in countries
like Iraq will continue throughout the twenty-first century.
Mohammad El Baradei, head of the U.N.'s International Atomic
Energy Agency, has observed that there is something of a
"WAL*MART" in the illegal trade of nuclear weapons technology.
Russia cannot account for much of its fissile material or many of
its nuclear scientists. No one knows where most of Iraq's nuclear
scientists have gone. Pakistani scientists are known to have sold
nuclear know-how to Libya, Iran, and North Korea. North Korea
has supplied Pakistan with the missile technology necessary to
launch a nuclear attack on India. Syria, Egypt, and Israel are all
believed to have chemical weapons. North Korea, now refining
its own uranium for nuclear bombs, is within artillery range of
Seoul, the capital city and largest population center of South
Korea. To launch a major nuclear assault on South Korea, it
would not even need missiles or an air force. Weapons of mass
destruction are no longer a preserve of the major powers, and a
nuclear war among emerging powers seems more than likely in
the coming years.

But the way to prevent war is *not* to start a war: Weapons of
mass destruction in a country like Iraq are a reason — *the reason*
— to develop a permanent structure of world peace. We should
take the problem seriously, as President Bush has said, but what
we should do about it is the opposite of war. War is a primitive,
reactionary response; this is a moment to respond creatively.
Weapons of mass destruction are the glaring proof that we have
to resolve conflicts peaceably, through stronger global institutions.
U.N. weapons inspectors should be in Iraq and in all nations,
including the United States, and should be given the respect and
authority to do their work. If intervention becomes necessary, it
should be undertaken by the world community *as a whole* and
not by any one nation or group of nations. The only legitimate

intervention in the internal affairs of a single nation is by the world as a unified body.

The U.N. must circumvent demand for chemical, biological, and nuclear weapons in emerging nations by providing these countries with the security they are trying to achieve on their own. Qazi Hussain Ahmed, a radical Muslim opposition leader, said of Pakistani nuclear scientists, "The nuclear heroes made these nuclear weapons for us — that's why India never dared to touch us." Pakistan should instead look to the United Nations for security. The U.N. must develop the power and authority to protect Pakistan from India, North Korea from South Korea and the United States, and Iraq, Syria, Egypt, Israel, Libya, and Iran from whomever it feels threatened by. These countries need global security, not national security. Nuclear weapons provide neither.

Weapons of mass destruction are the moving force behind the evolution of a system of global security; it is the threat they pose to the continued existence of human civilization that makes the trend toward global sovereignty inevitable. We will have world government or no world at all. But there is no inevitable *path* to global unity. World government could evolve from a single national power such as the United States, from an oligarchy of national powers such as NATO, or from an international body such as the United Nations. If it evolves from the U.N., that body's mandate will have to become *supra*national as opposed to *inter*national. International organizations such as the Quintuple Alliance, the League of Nations, and the current United Nations are designed to maintain order without disturbing the national prerogative to destroy it. They are created by member nations not to limit national sovereignty but to preserve it. They represent national interests and not popular interests: Individual people are not members and have no direct voice. Internationalism is an important step toward globalism, but international organizations are not sovereign bodies and do not have the power to enforce international peace.

As we have seen, history shows that international organizations are established after major world wars. In periods of exhaustion and resolution following long years of destruction, major powers are willing — temporarily — to sacrifice some independence in the name of peace. Each emerging international organization is marginally more effective than its predecessor. The trend is hopeful, but it will not save us from war in the nuclear age. It is too slow. In the current age, we cannot wait for another round of general warfare to set up yet another international organization, even if it proves slightly better than the one we already have. International organizations will never establish permanent global peace because they do not get at the root cause of war. The root cause of war is the division of political sovereignty. As long as nations are politically divided, there will be war between them. *To look for a continuation of harmony among a number of independent, unconnected sovereignties situated in the same neighborhood would be to disregard the uniform course of human events and to set at defiance the accumulated experience of the ages.*[4] We must look beyond mere internationalism to globalism.

Aware of the technological imperative behind the trend toward globalism, we will be in a position to divert the flow of sovereignty to creative directions as nuclear crises arise. Thinking outside of the national box, we may be able to avoid the pitfalls of an oppressive United Nations or an imperialist United States. With ingenuity and good timing, the United Nations will be reconstituted in a manner that represents the world's peoples directly and democratically. It will become a truly global body with direct popular representation and a home for the emerging soul of a united humanity. There is no reason why this should not happen, but it will happen only if people make it happen. It is not inevitable. There is nothing inevitable about liberty, equality, and justice.

Sovereignty is the right to use violence. Who, then, do we trust with that right? To whom do we give the power of death that we might live? In the past we have chosen people who look and act and think the way we do. But now we are forced to choose again. In unity, we redefine who we are and grant sovereignty, as a gift, to ourselves.

Survival is a function not of strength but of adaptability to conditions as they are.

Part ll — The Practical

5. The Kyoto Protocol

THE ENVIRONMENTAL MOVEMENT OF THE 1970s WAS CON-
cerned primarily with local and national issues: recycling, insecti-
cides, habitat destruction, litter control, and air and water pollution. These were mostly municipal and national issues that could
be handled by existing government entities. In the 1980s and
1990s, issues arose concerning the earth's atmosphere, and a
new awareness emerged on the global level. Concern became
worldwide and local at the same time. There was a recognized
need for a common understanding of the human relationship to
the rest of the living world. The deterioration of the atmosphere
and the weather — and of the biosphere as a whole — heightened awareness around the world of what human beings were
doing wrong and what they needed to be doing right. This was
not just another new issue; it was a global alarm that called for
drastic and immediate measures to preserve life on Earth. It was a
big-picture scenario that required an expansion of human consciousness, a reorganization of human life, and a redefinition of
being human. The atmosphere had wrapped and shielded us for
so long that we no longer noticed it and had forgotten to care for
it. Now the earth's blanket was coming loose. We were all in
great peril — and in it *together*.

The first big scare was a measurable destruction of ozone in
the upper atmosphere. (In the lower atmosphere ozone is a pol-
lutant, but in the upper atmosphere, it becomes a life-protecting
shield against ultraviolet radiation.) Chlorofluorocarbons — or

CFCs — used in refrigerants and aerosol cans, were escaping into the atmosphere and breaking down the earth's natural protection against harmful radiation. This affects all forms of life, not only human. CFCs break down oxygen molecules in their triatomic form (O_3, or "ozone") into the more common diatomic (O_2) form, which lets ultraviolet radiation through to the earth's surface. The problem is that CFC molecules are catalysts: They break down one oxygen molecule after another without being consumed in the process and so remain in the upper atmosphere doing their dirty work for hundreds of years. As more and more are released, more and more ozone is destroyed, and more damage is done to the earth's plants, animals, and humans. A team of British scientists was able to detect and measure an expanding "hole" in the ozone over Antarctica as increasing rates of skin cancer were being reported all over the world. This was an environmental disaster of unprecedented proportions. Everyone was affected at the same time and in the same way. This was not just a fish kill or a few days of urban smog; this was a threat to the living world as a whole, a potential *un*-creation of what was given us. We were inflicting destruction on the entire planet for the sake of air-conditioning and hair spray.

But it never got that bad. The initiative in the fight against CFCs was taken by the producers themselves — the chemical industry. The potential disaster was so frightening and the problem so directly attributed to a particular family of chemicals that the industry knew that at the very least it had a severe public relations problem on its hands. It knew better than to resist the regulation of CFCs. Dupont Chemical took the lead. As the leading producer of CFCs, it was in the best position to limit production, and, because only about ten percent of its sales were linked to them, it was not dependent on CFCs to stay in business. The fact that it was already researching alternatives would put it in a competitive position — even with an outright ban. Dupont also knew that consumers tend to absolve themselves of complicity in environmental problems by blaming producers, even as they continue to consume. But Dupont, willing as it was to make a sacrifice, could not effectively do it alone. If it were to stop production unilaterally other companies would step in and fill the demand for aerosols and refrigerants, and the problem would only get worse. But because the problem involved the atmosphere, even a total ban by the U.S. Environmental Protection Agency would not have been of value because production would shift overseas. Global action was required, and global action taken.

The United Nations sponsored a series of conferences culminating in the Montreal Protocol of 1987. The nations of the world, with the cooperation of industry, agreed to reduce drastically and eventually to eliminate all production of CFCs. Everyone recognized the seriousness of the problem and did the right thing. The only contention was between the industrialized nations — "The North" — and developing nations — "The South." Nations in the process of increasing their own standard of living insisted on reserving the right to compromise the environment in the name of economic development, as had wealthier nations before them. Temporary limited production of CFCs was thus allowed in some countries, with the assurance that alternative refrigerants and aerosols would soon be available.

The Montreal Protocol has proven an enormous success. CFC production has plummeted, and the "hole in the ozone" is already showing signs of decreasing. Ultraviolet radiation will remain elevated over much of the earth's surface for years to come, but the trend is toward recovery. The problem, however drastic and life threatening, was relatively simple: It involved one substance that could be replaced. More important from the standpoint of public opinion, the science was simple: We knew what the problem was, where it came from, and how to fix it. There was a direct cause-and-effect relation between what we were doing to the environment and what we could expect to see happen as a result. The problem was caused by human intervention and could be resolved by human intervention. We learned from Montreal that national governments, in the floodlight of world public opinion, will cooperate to resolve global environmental emergencies. Industry will also cooperate if it is allowed to participate in developing new rules of the game. Most important, we learned that science can save us from inadvertently destroying ourselves. We need people out there watching things like holes in the ozone. Scientists should continue to be free to explore and examine and measure things that have no apparent practical application. They should play in the sandbox — and get paid for it — only incidentally keeping track of where we are and what we are doing to the environment.

While ozone depletion is a fairly straightforward problem with a simple solution, the second global atmospheric scare — climate change — is extremely complicated and has no simple solution. Human beings appear to be inadvertently changing the earth's temperature, rainfall, storm patterns, forest cover, ocean currents, and sea level through the release of "greenhouse gases" into the atmosphere. Carbon dioxide (CO_2), methane (CH_4), nitrous oxide (N_2O), water vapor (H_2O), and several other less abundant atmospheric gases (including the same CFCs that cause ozone depletion) trap heat in the earth's atmosphere by allowing sunlight to pass through to the earth's surface but not allowing reflected radiation to pass back through to space. This is called the "greenhouse effect." Glass on a greenhouse does the same thing. You may notice the greenhouse effect when you leave your car closed up on a sunny day: Temperatures inside the car become much higher than outside. Greenhouse gases do to the earth what your windshield does to the seat upholstery. They make the earth much warmer than it would otherwise be. This is a good thing, and a natural thing, because the earth would be a much colder and more hostile environment without them. The complication is that all these gases (with the exception of CFCs and a few others) are natural; what is *un*natural is their heightened concentration due to human activity. The concentration of carbon dioxide, in particular, is now more than 30 percent higher than it was before human industry began burning coal and petroleum and releasing vast quantities of CO_2 into the air. More greenhouse gas means more heat in the earth's atmosphere, and more heat means more climate change. This means higher temperatures in certain parts of the world, higher sea levels (as ice caps melt and ocean waters expand with higher temperatures), changes in the frequency and severity of storms and droughts, changes in weather patterns and ocean currents, and even mass extinctions as climatic conditions fluctuate beyond the tolerance of endangered species. But nobody knows to what extent the climate has already changed nor to what extent the change is our fault. There are natural variations in climate, and we may be seeing something that would be happening without us and that we cannot correct.

Greenhouse gases have been understood for many years, and it has been known for many years that human industry has increased their concentrations in the atmosphere. Since the late 1800s, there have been speculations that they may be causing climate change. But proof of climate change and of its link to human activity is difficult to establish. There can be no absolute certainty for either of these — at least, not yet. *Climate* is, by definition, an average condition of the weather over many years. But *how* many years? A hot year or even a series of hot years is not a climate change: The following years may be quite cold. Year-to-year temperature fluctuations are common and natural within a stable climate; therefore, establishing actual climate change beyond doubt takes many years. The number of years depends on the definition of *climate*. One can claim a stable climate after any number of hot years by simply extending the baseline definition of *climate*. There is always the chance that colder years will follow. "Proof" of climate change can be postponed in this way for as long as seems convenient. And even if the climate is shown to be changing, establishing a link to human activity is even more difficult.

Unlike ozone depletion, climate is not a simple, linear system. There are numerous factors involved in how it works and how it changes, and there is no direct cause-and-effect relation between what we see happening and what we are doing. We cannot say for certain that human-produced greenhouse emissions have caused climate to change. In Montreal, it was easy to establish that the atmosphere was affected by CFCs, and it was easy to link them to human activity (in that humans were their sole source). Unlike CFCs, only a relatively small part of the total greenhouse gases in the atmosphere are man-made; their effect on the climate is marginal and not easily isolated from natural causes. Even if climate changes are detected, they could be due to other causes.

But despite the impossibility of absolute certainty, scientists now believe that the climate *is* changing and that we are causing it to change. Consensus for climate change and for its anthropogenic origins was established during the 1990s — the hottest (temperature) decade in recorded history. In its Second Assessment Report, the United Nations Intergovernmental Panel on Climate Change stated that greenhouse gases have risen and continue to rise as a result of human activities, that global temperatures have risen, that sea levels have risen, and that the evidence suggests a discernible human influence on global climate. The report went on to state that the current trend is toward reduced biodiversity; altered growing seasons; boundary shifts between grasslands, forests, and scrublands; hotter deserts and increased desertification; loss of one third to one half of the earth's glacier mass; coastal erosion and flooding; and changes in ocean circulation and sea ice with major impacts on marine ecosystems.[5]

There were scientists who disagreed with the consensus. Some felt that the links were not strong enough to be positively identified, and others felt there were no links at all. Some outside the scientific community — including fossil fuel-based industry groups,

anti-environmentalists, and libertarian "pro-enterprise" groups —
have seized on lingering uncertainties in the scientific community
to claim that the problem does not exist or that there is not
enough evidence to do anything about it, especially anything
expensive.

But the consensus is strong — as strong as it can be until further evidence is gathered. It is strong enough for the world to
begin working on solutions, and the world has, in fact, gone to
work on the problem of climate change. One reason work has
begun without absolute proof is that, like a growing cancer, global
warming is most easily treated in its early stages. If we wait for
twenty or thirty years until we are *sure* the climate is changing —
and that we are the ones causing it — it may be too late to correct it. A habitable climate is a narrow range between extremes of
heat and cold, flood and drought. It is a balancing act, much like
that of balancing a broomstick in the palm of your hand. It will
stay upright only if kept close to vertical. You can keep it upright
so long as only minor adjustments are needed, but if you allow it
to fall too far in any direction, you cannot save it no matter how fast
you run. Accordingly, the world decided that it was worth looking
into the problem of climate change at the Earth Summit of 1992
in Rio de Janeiro. The U.N. framework Convention on Climate
Control was adopted at that meeting, and groundwork for specific
measures against greenhouse emissions was established in 1997
at a conference in Kyoto, Japan. The Kyoto Protocol, which established who was to do what in the effort to prevent a runaway climate, emerged from that conference and was signed the following
year by more than 160 nations, including the United States.

The terms of the Kyoto Protocol require cutbacks in carbon
emissions only in the industrialized nations; the developing
countries, whose emissions are significantly lower, are allowed to
keep polluting for the time being. This is because the rich countries developed their economies with cheap energy and polluted

the atmosphere for centuries — it would be unfair at this point to impose higher energy costs on countries now in the process of early economic development. The North is, after all, responsible for the current elevated levels of greenhouse gases; why should the South have to pay? There is justice to this, and the initial concessions made by the industrial countries at Kyoto reflect it. But the problem with Kyoto is that developing countries do not have enough incentive to begin the development process in a carbon-efficient manner. In fact, if the emission allowances they are eventually given are based on how much they have polluted up to that point (as they were for the industrialized countries), the developing countries have an incentive to *maximize* emissions until then. There are provisions (the CDM, or Clean Development Mechanism) that allow industrialized nations to gain additional emission credits by assisting developing countries with clean energy projects, but no one is sure how, or if, this will work. Developing countries themselves gain no emission credits by participating (and are not bound by them in any case), and developed countries may find this a convenient way to increase their own emissions within the system. Because the system sets the interests of the North against those of the South, it has the effect of further dividing the poor countries from the rich. It does not take full advantage of the fact that all people are in this together. It would be better if a simpler, more just, and equitable system were devised where all countries and all people were to play by the same rules.

The Kyoto agreement sets a baseline for emissions standards at 1990 levels. A standard has to be established and, given the many years of hard bargaining leading up to Kyoto, we are lucky that anything was agreed at all. But establishing a "right to pollute" based on past levels of pollution favors the worst offenders of the past, particularly the former Soviet bloc countries. Russia and Ukraine were probably the least energy-efficient countries in the world in 1990, but with the fall of the Soviet Union and the consequent economic collapse in Eastern Europe, they now have much lower emissions. They were not trying to save energy or reduce greenhouse emissions — their economies just slowed way down. But now they are rewarded for their wastefulness in the past with more emissions permits than they can use, which they will probably sell to the United States at high prices.

A more equitable system for allowable emissions would be based on population. This has been suggested by African delegations to Kyoto and supported by India and China. Rather than starting out with existing pollution levels, why not begin with acceptable levels of greenhouse gases for the earth as a whole — now and over the next several decades — and then distribute the right to emit these gases on a per capita basis? Every man, woman, and child will have the same right to alter the atmosphere and endanger the earth's climatic stability, regardless of who they are, what country they live in, and how developed their economy is. Emission permits could still be distributed through national governments, with the more populous countries receiving more permits. Everybody everywhere would have the same incentive to develop new energy-efficient technologies, to switch to alternative fuels, and to reduce their consumption of fossil fuels in any way they find most efficient. Developing countries would, of course, benefit initially. With higher populations and lower per capita energy use, they would have emissions permits to sell to the industrialized nations at whatever price the market would bear. This would give them the capital they need for health care, education, and infrastructure, and for other types of environmental protection. To keep from consuming their own carbon credits in the process of development, they would have great incentive to use the most carbon-efficient technologies available. This would spur the market in the industrialized countries for new energy technology.

A per capita-based emissions policy is unlikely to happen anytime soon. It would involve too great a concession on the part of the North at this time and would require a much more profound linkage between global environmental policy and economic development. But the concept is not as far-fetched as it may seem. There is already a profound linkage between the global environment and economic development that appears on the world stage whenever environmental issues are discussed. The "right to development" of poor countries was firmly established at the Rio Conference in 1992, as was the commitment of the world environmental community to the "development and environmental needs of present and future generations." Industrialized countries are increasingly aware of global economic injustice, and industries themselves are increasingly aware of sacrifices they will have to make for the environment. According to the Kyoto agreement as it now stands, American utility companies are already required to spend millions, perhaps hundreds of millions, on emissions permits from Russia and Ukraine and have already begun preliminary negotiations to secure them. Industry would accept a per capita emissions basis — even if it were expensive — as long as it is given the chance to compete and make a profit on a fair and equitable basis. What industry does *not* want is a clumsy and lopsided bureaucratic system that wastes time, money, and human initiative. Eventually, countries like the United States, Japan, and Europe will accept the idea of per capita emissions rights because it will be simple, equitable, and market-directed, and everyone will be playing by the same rules.

From an environmental standpoint, a single per capita basis will be better suited to the actual process of greenhouse gas reduction. A realistic global emissions level can be set based on scientific research and emissions certificates issued only for that amount. Year-by-year flexibility can be built into the system, but a single global level can be established for each year (or each five years) and established above the fray of international politics. As the system now stands, bargaining for increased emissions rights is likely to go on indefinitely. Each country will claim that it is treated unfairly, that it has a special situation that needs addressing, or that some other country or countries had an unfair advantage when emissions levels were initially established. There will be constant upward pressure on each nation's emissions level, and the overall level is likely to fluctuate more according to the political climate in the meeting room than to the global climate out-of-doors.

The emissions trading system established with the Kyoto Protocol is based on American experience with a similar trading program in sulfur dioxide emissions provided by 1990 amendment to the Clean Air Act. Many environmentalists were initially repulsed by the idea of selling the right to pollute, but the system is a good idea and has worked quite well, at least within national boundaries. The actual cost of reducing emissions has turned out to be much less than anticipated. Basically, what emissions trading says is that the responsibility for compromising environmental health should be shared by the actual polluter *and* those who create the economic demand that results in pollution. Whether or not they are its direct cause, those who benefit from pollution should help clean it up. It is too easy to say that acid precipitation or CFC contamination is caused by utilities and chemical companies: Utilities and chemical companies do what we, as consumers, want them to do. They do what we tell them to do with our dollars. If we were not there to buy electricity and air conditioners, they would stop polluting tomorrow. They have no interest in burning coal or producing refrigerants for their own sake. We want what they have to offer, and we must either stop wanting it or improve the means by which we get it. In wanting electric lights and refrigerators and automobiles, it is the consumer who is compromising the environment.

Emissions trading also says that there is room within the biosphere for a certain level of certain types of human activity. Emissions trading is not appropriate for CFCs because there is no acceptable level of ozone destruction — but it *is* appropriate for carbon. We can keep burning coal and gasoline and keep cutting down trees to some extent. The question is, To what extent? How much is it worth to us to keep the climate stable and protect the forests? It is worth nothing to us if we blame it on industry, because we are simply passing on the cost. We are telling them to pay as if we had no part in it. By admitting that we are all compromising the environment when we turn on a light or drive to work or buy an air conditioner, we have to ask ourselves questions that are more likely to get real answers. Trading for the right to pollute, then, as mercenary as it sounds, is a much more realistic way of dealing with environmental pollution than pointing the finger at a smokestack and saying Stop! The principle of establishing acceptable emissions levels forces us to see what we are doing and what can be done in a more practical manner.

Who does the actual polluting does not matter; by allowing the right to trade pollution rights, we give real financial incentives to companies to reduce pollution. They will make money by behaving properly. If there is still too much pollution, acceptable levels can be lowered. Fewer permits will be issued, making each one worth that much more. The cost of pollution will thereby increase to the point where, from a business standpoint, changes will *have* to be made. Trading, I think, should be extended to other areas of environmental protection, such as forest conservation. We all love trees and hate to see them cut down, but we also like to live in houses. If sustainable lumber yields could be established on a worldwide, national, and local basis, lumber companies would have to buy the right to cut down trees, and you and I would have to pay higher prices for the houses we live in for the sake of the trees we love. Environmental protection will have to be worth this much to be realized in the real world.

The other great advantage of the trading system is that it is the way industry likes to operate. Industry is more likely to "buy into" a system that gives them freedom to make their own decisions based on good business practice. They can decide for themselves whether to buy more emissions certificates from some other part of the world or to build new, more energy-efficient production facilities. Because operating decisions will be market driven rather than imposed by government regulation, industry will not have to focus attention on understanding and complying with ever-changing sets of bureaucratic procedures. They will be able to do what they do best: make a profit. They will be allowed to make for us what we want within a market-driven system that rewards sound environmental practices.

But the real weakness of the global emissions trading system proposed at Kyoto — whether based on 1990 levels of carbon emissions or on population — is that it requires a strong international legal system that does not yet exist. The sulfur dioxide trading system within the United States, upon which the global system is based, operates under the guarantee of the federal government. The American government created the system, administers it under the Clean Air Act, and enforces compliance through the Environmental Protection Agency. Companies know that they have to comply, their competitors have to comply, and that everybody will have to keep complying next year and the year after. They buy and sell sulfur emissions permits with the assurance that they will be valid. They have begun, therefore, to look at them as property rights. For x dollars, they have the right to release y number of tons of sulfur into the air.

But property rights — all property rights — are only as good as the government that guarantees them. You may not think of this every time you open your front door, but your right to walk into the house is only as good as a piece of paper in the county courthouse. You pay a lot of money for that piece of paper, and if you find that someone else has moved into your house while you were gone, you will want the government to honor it. You will want the government to guarantee the piece of paper that gives you the right you have purchased. The same is true with emissions permits. They are just pieces of paper guaranteed by a government. A company will only pay for one if it knows that it cannot pollute without it and that other companies have to pay for them also. If the legal system is weak, if enforcement is lax, if too many permits are issued, or if counterfeit permits are issued or bribes taken, the system will collapse. More important, if anyone has the right to pull out of the system whenever they choose, there will be uncertainty as to whether there is any value at all to a permit. Why should my company or my nation comply with very expensive emissions reductions if yours does not? Why should I buy something for several million dollars that may not have any meaning?

The system as proposed at Kyoto depends on the current structure of international law, which is weak by any standard. It depends on a subject nation to recognize its jurisdiction at its own discretion; it has no means of independent enforcement. It depends on countries to police themselves. The current system of international law is also geared mostly toward bilateral conflict resolution — that is, toward resolving conflicts between two contending powers rather than toward creating overall policy. Environmental legal disputes are multilateral by nature and require the kind of global overview that does not yet exist in international arenas. The proper mechanisms of enforcement simply do not yet exist for the Kyoto Protocol. The international trading system it mandates will be based on a concept of international property whose value remains questionable. For instance, a company operating in the United States will need to continue to burn coal in the near future to supply its customers with electricity and remain in business. To do so, it will have to buy carbon emissions certificates from the U.S. government. But because the U.S. is currently far behind the rest of world in reducing emissions, there will not be enough certificates to meet domestic needs. The company will therefore have to buy its permit overseas (or the U.S. government will buy it for them). This will be expensive and create the incentive to switch to lower carbon or non-carbon fuels. But if it buys the certificates, it will want to know that they are valid and that competitors have to make the same expenditures and are subject to the same rules.

Likewise, the U.S. government, as it watches millions and perhaps billions of its dollars flowing to other countries for emissions certificates, will want to be sure that other countries are complying with the system. Your emissions certificate is a property right that must be ensured against the claims of others in order to have any value at all. Both private industry and the national government will want an effective inspection system that will ensure the value of what they are purchasing. If the Kyoto agreement retains its current treaty form, it will depend on too weak a system of international law. It depends on nations choosing to stay in the system, which they may not do. An individual country may decide that it is better off *individually* outside the system even if everyone is better off *collectively* inside it. As soon as a country feels that its separate interest overtakes its share of collective interests, it is likely to drop out, and as soon as one drops out, others are likely to follow. As a private company or as a national government, the last thing you want to find out after you have spent millions of dollars on emissions rights is that other countries are pulling out of the system. Until a more advanced system of enforced international law is established, this uncertainty will undermine confidence in emissions trading, and the system is unlikely to work.

In the short run — that is, in the next decade or so — Kyoto will work only with American participation. America is the worst polluter in the world in both absolute and per capita terms. With four percent of the world's population, it dumps about twenty-five percent of the world's carbon pollution into the air. As the world's military, economic, and political superpower, the U.S. has enormous bargaining power at international conferences of all kinds. Almost all the terms that emerged from Kyoto were those insisted on by the United States. After two and a half years of intense negotiation culminating in a twelve-day climax in Japan involving more than ten thousand people, an agreement was worked out in which America got what it wanted. It signed the treaty but has since turned its back on it. The U.S. Senate has refused to ratify it. The current U.S. presidential administration (George W. Bush) has established an energy policy clearly favorable to the coal and petroleum industries and has announced its intentions to ignore the terms of the Kyoto Protocol. (The Bush Administration's Energy Policy Statement of 2003 made no mention of the Kyoto Protocol, CO_2 emissions reductions, or climate change and included federal subsidies for nuclear and fossil fuels industries.)

The world needs leadership in environmental protection. But Americans, for the most part, do not understand the position they are in and do not want the leadership that has been thrust upon them. Most are unaware it exists. They are proud of the global power America has but do not seem to appreciate the responsibilities it entails. Many have a simplistic view of world affairs: What's good for America is what America should be striving for. There is very little understanding of global citizenship. The current presidential administration exemplifies this attitude quite well.

The Bush Administration understands the role of government to be the creation of a favorable climate for business. Commercial prosperity, if allowed to take its natural course, will create the economic surpluses necessary to pay for government, education, charity, and environmental protection. Those who create the surplus will be in the best position to know how to use it wisely. It is an old idea of government — a legitimate one — and one that should always be kept in mind when dealing with questions of how best to make an economic system work. Business, after all, has been the driving engine of modern human civilization.

But it is an idea of government that does not accept the general welfare of humanity as its primary principle. It is a reactionary idea of government that is unlikely to consider creative approaches to new realities. The Kyoto Protocol involves too great a change in the fundamental concept of government and too great a

commitment to nonprofit-related values for the current administration to consider in any depth. It is just too big for them to understand, much less pay for.

What the world now has is environmental leadership without
a leader. It has looked to American science and American initiative to make things happen, but it sees the cold face of
isolationism and indifference. This is hard for the rest of the
world to understand. There are good reasons for American rejection of Kyoto — and bad reasons as well. The good reasons are
that it discriminates between rich and poor countries, it does not
apply everywhere, and it establishes an emissions trading system
that is unlikely to succeed. The bad reasons for rejecting the
treaty are that it will require financial sacrifice on the part of
industry and government and that it implies an admission, on the
part of those who prefer to believe otherwise, that global
warming actually exists. But what many in the American government fear most is that Kyoto's effective implementation will mean
a system of international law that will further erode the principle
of independent national sovereignty.

Current administration policy, however, constitutes what I
would call political *weather*, not political *climate*. Political
weather changes from year to year and term to term but averages
out over time — that is, an environmentally friendly administration is followed by an environmentally destructive one and back
again. The political weather will change in time — an American
administration will one day come to accept the Kyoto Protocol or
something like it. But even a change in political weather will not
be enough to address the root problems of the earth's environment.
A much deeper change will have to come in how people understand their presence in the environment and how they might
reorganize themselves within it. If the climate of the earth is
changing and not just its weather, the earth's political climate will
have to change, too. New sets of questions will have to be asked
and answered in a larger context of being and doing. Grappling

with the climate problem will fundamentally change our understanding of what can be done by whom, as will so many other coming global issues, including arms control, labor legislation, trade, law enforcement, economic development, and terrorism. Regulating the earth's atmosphere is not an international issue but a global one that will require a global response. We will have to see ourselves in the air together and respond to the wholeness of the atmosphere with our own wholeness.

Kyoto is as good as it could possibly be at this point. It is a recognition of global responsibility. It is the first time that national governments — with the help of industry and nongovernment environmental groups — have established legally binding quantified constraints on emissions. It is part of an ongoing historical trend, however slow, toward a full understanding of how we are affecting the planet we live on and what we should be doing about it for ourselves and for succeeding generations. Its importance goes beyond establishing levels for emissions and goes beyond lowering emissions to setting up a rudimentary system for managing human activities in relation to the atmosphere as a whole. The system is unlikely to work well in the immediate future, but when the time comes to act we will be in a better position to do so. We will have had experience in managing emissions on a global scale. Much will be learned about how well the system does and does not work, and that can be applied to all areas of environmental protection.

Given the current political values in the United States and elsewhere, it is amazing that there is any international environmental system at all. Kyoto will depend on an extended, updated, perhaps revolutionary new system of international law — a system that may bridge the gap between international and truly global law. This is a good thing.

6. The Law of the Sea

NATIONALISM IS A TERRESTRIAL CONCEPT THAT LOSES ITS
consistency when mixed with water. It is unclear what should be
done about it once the dry land is left behind. But a ghostly sort
of national sovereignty inhabits immediate coastal areas in the
form of *territorial seas*. These are waters adjacent to national shore-
lines that lie within the range of shore-based cannon fire, usually
extending about three nautical miles into the open ocean. Here
the nation–state reaches out to claim the water as it claimed the
land. The high seas beyond belong to nobody. Nationality makes
little sense beyond a few miles from the land's edge, where water
is just what lies between pieces of land. Even naval power is an
extension of terrestrial power in that its intention is not to own
water but to attack or defend shore installations and passages
between shore installations. This is the way it has always been —
until recently.

It has been this way because the industrialized maritime nations
have preferred to keep it so. By belonging to no one, the oceans
have been open to those in the best position to use them. The
United States, the former Soviet Union, Japan, Great Britain, and
other Western European nations have been content to leave the
oceans open and free to fishing, commercial shipping, and naval
patrol because de facto control of the high seas by countries with
large navies and merchant marines is preferable to interference
by smaller, non-maritime nations with less direct interest. Until
recently, the oceans have been large enough for everyone and

roomy enough to resolve conflicts on a bilateral or regional basis without resort to an overall global regime. But the discoveries of offshore oil reserves and deep-sea mineral beds have changed the legal status of the oceans. Oceanic oil spills and dwindling fish harvests have changed its environmental status. There is now a consensus in the world that the seventy-two percent of the earth's surface that is covered by water belongs not to nobody — but to everybody. The United Nations Conventions on the Law of the Sea have been an attempt to speak to that consensus.

The movement to internationalize the oceans was begun inadvertently by the United States in 1945. President Truman proclaimed that his nation held the exclusive right to explore and exploit mineral resources on the continental shelf surrounding the United States. This was a unilateral act not intended to affect anything beyond the national interests of the United States. However, it applied to an area far beyond the then-accepted three-mile limit of territorial waters. It was an enormous extension of national sovereignty into international waters. The United States was primarily interested in petroleum, but there was no reason to interpret the Truman proclamation as limited to petroleum. It might apply to fishing rights, navigation, and other mineral resources. The world's seabeds were known to be littered with manganese nodules, and there were any number of other untold mineral riches in the oceans open to whoever got there first. Some countries were anxious to maintain fishing rights off their own shores.

Within the next two years, sensing an impending race to claim oceanic resources, Argentina, Mexico, Chile, and Peru claimed territorial waters extending two hundred miles from their coastlines. Countries in Africa and Asia followed suit. Everyone wanted as big a share as they could grab, and there was talk of drawing lines down the middle of all the world's oceans and dividing up the *entire surface* of the earth among coastal states. This prospect scared landlocked and "geographically disadvantaged" states with limited coastlines. There was great concern within the United Nations that the "land grab" of the oceans would get out of hand — that the less advantaged nations would lose out and that there might be conflicts among the larger nations. The first and second U.N. Conventions on the Law of the Sea were held in 1958 and 1960 to promote an orderly international procedure for exploitation of ocean resources, but a comprehensive plan was not adopted by the United Nations until 1982 at the third U.N. convention (UNCLOS III).

Malta's U.N. ambassador, Arvid Pardo, stated in a 1967 speech to the U.N. General Assembly that the seabed and ocean floor should be declared the "common heritage of mankind." This distinctly global principle inspired the next fifteen years of negotiations but did not, unfortunately, survive them. The United Nations Third Convention on the Law of the Sea began work in 1973 in New York, then moved on to Caracas and Geneva and Montego Bay, Jamaica, where the final draft was signed in 1982 by 117 nations. Seventeen nations, most of them European, abstained from voting on the treaty, and four voted against it: Israel, Turkey, Venezuela, and the United States.

The major issues of UNCLOS III were fishing, navigation, deep-sea mineral extraction, offshore oil, and pollution control. The most tangible outcome of the convention was recognition by the U.N. of the right of coastal states to declare territorial waters of up to twelve nautical miles and Exclusive Economic Zones (EEZs) of up to two hundred nautical miles off their coastlines. A nation could maintain all "sovereign rights" in its territorial waters and all rights to ocean resources, living and mineral, within its EEZ. Other nations maintained the right to navigation and overflight in EEZs as long as their presence constituted "innocent passage." The common heritage of mankind was pushed out past the two-hundred-mile limit. Landlocked and geographically disadvantaged nations were left with a vague promise to a share of this domain and to an ill-defined share of the "unused portions" of the EEZs of neighboring coastal states. The treaty is a clear statement of the principle of international law on the high seas but is also a clear partition of the world's commons into separate national properties. Ninety percent of the earth's living marine resources and nearly all its known oil reserves are concentrated on continental shelves within the two-hundred-mile EEZs of coastal states. Most of the earth's water surface remained the common heritage of mankind, but almost all of its wealth fell within the hands of separate nations, their share depending on the accidents of geography. UNCLOS III was a statement by the United Nations that the oceans belonged to everyone, although clearly more to some than to others.

The United States never accepted even this principle. The Nixon, Ford, and Carter administrations maintained an active team at U.N. sea conferences throughout the 1970's. But in March 1981, after eight years of negotiating with 130 other nations of the world and two days before one of the final sessions was to begin, the Reagan administration fired nearly the entire U.S. delegation. A smaller team of negotiators was chosen, most of them unfamiliar with the proceedings to date. The new team presented a list of U.S. objections to the draft convention and refused to make compromises. When the final product emerged, the U.S. team voted against it. U.S. objections had to do with seabed mining, claiming that freedom of the high seas meant that the U.S. or anyone else should have the right to mine anything anywhere at any time. This "Wild West" view put forward by the American delegation was vigorously denounced by nearly every other delegation present, claiming that seabed minerals fell under the common heritage principle that had inspired the original Law of the Sea convention.

The U.S. delegation had reasons to shun the U.N. Law of the Sea. From its own purely nationalist perspective, the new content had little to offer the United States. Agreements concerning navigation and territorial waters could be maintained with other nations on a bilateral and regional basis on terms favorable to U.S. interests. If other nations attempted to block shipping channels through narrow straits such as Gibraltar or Malacca, the U.S. could find alternate routes or force its way through, if necessary. Even strategic nuclear interests could be maintained without the treaty: The new Trident submarine, with its stock of more accurate and longer-range missiles, could reach vital targets in the Soviet Union without having to navigate as close to its borders as did the old Polaris and Poseidon submarines. With the power of its navy and coast guard, the U.S. could claim de facto rights to off-shore oil and mineral deposits without U.N. guarantees of these rights vis-à-vis other nations. The prevailing attitude of the American delegation was that the seas did not belong to everybody nor did they belong to nobody: They belonged to anybody. More particularly, they belonged to anybody with naval power. As one speaker at the forum on the UNCLOS III sponsored by the American Enterprise Institute said:

> Do not create this creature. Why is it in the American international interest to interpose this new obstacle to the free access by American consumers to the remaining resources of the world that are not now locked up by governments hostile to the interest of our consumers? ... Free access, to me the common heritage of mankind, is a continuing right of free and nondiscriminatory access, free of price control, free of production control, free of restraints of accommodation and restraint of trade. We are getting exactly the reverse of that if we create this hostile supergovernment. Do not do it. On day one of the resumption of the negotiations, say "I am very sorry. We neglected to withdraw this 1970 treaty from the table. We are withdrawing it now."[6]

The U.S. finally signed UNCLOS III in 1994, but the U.S. Senate has not yet (at this writing) ratified it, and we are not bound by it. Enough other nations (sixty) have ratified the treaty, however, and it is now binding on them. It is unlikely that it will be ratified by the United States anytime soon.

But is the Law of the Sea worth fighting for from the global point of view? The only truly global accomplishment of the convention was the prevention of a complete median-line partitioning of the oceans into national spheres of exploitation. Its environmental accomplishments are virtually nonexistent. There is no provision for overall environmental protection for fish, seabirds, crustaceans, whales, coral reefs, or other marine organisms. There are no worldwide regulations to prevent oil spills or other forms of ocean pollution from commercial and military vessels, much less to prevent the eighty percent of ocean pollution that originates on land. Instead, coastal states are "free" to establish their own environmental laws and fishing limits within their own Exclusive Economic Zones. But these are not to interfere with economic development or commercial shipping, and military vessels are *explicitly exempt* from any environmental regulation. Fish and marine mammals are addressed as "living resources" and are considered only in terms of their economic value to humans. The general attitude presented to the world by UNCLOS III is not one of care or protection — much less of relating to the organic wholeness of the ocean — but of use and exploitation. The only questions the convention even begins to resolve are those related to who exploits what.

Globalism can be defined as an understanding of the world as greater than the sum of its parts. *Internationalism* understands the whole to be equal to its parts. The Law of the Sea is, by these definitions, very much an international treaty. Designed to forestall a free-for-all on the world's commons, it has accomplished at least part of the international mission it was given by channeling and coordinating national self-interests. It has overseen an orderly two-hundred-mile expansion of national sovereignty into the seas. But it has done virtually nothing to prepare humanity for the commercial and environmental realities of the twenty-first century. As world trade and industrial production expand and as sea plants and animals and the chemistry of seawater itself change in response to human presence, the oceans will become a lake within the realm of human civilization. We will have to reexamine the wisdom of carving the lake up into parts that reflect our own divisions.

7. Maquiladoras

MAQUILA FACTORIES, OR "MAQUILADORAS," LINE MEXICO'S northern frontier in Tijuana, Mexicali, Nogales, Ciudad Juarez, Reynosa, and Matamoros — some of them within view of the American border. Thousands of trucks laden with raw textiles, electronic components, chemicals, and auto parts cross the southern border from the U.S. every day, and thousands more with finished apparel, circuit boards, appliances, wiring harnesses, and furniture pass north. From the standpoint of the Mexican government and American capital, it is a win–win situation: Taxes are collected in Mexico for the valued added, jobs are provided for otherwise unemployed Mexican workers, and hard currency is generated to pay for imports while American businesses profit enormously in the form of cheap, nonorganized labor. The only losers are labor and the environment.

Maquila is a Spanish word referring to the portion of the farmer's grain kept by the miller after it has been ground into flour. The farmer never gives up possession of his goods, though he does sacrifice a portion to the miller for value added. The word now also applies to a special program devised by the Mexican government whereby foreign components are brought into Mexico duty-free and assembled into finished products by Mexican labor so long as the finished product is reexported. The components and finished products never enter the Mexican economy and never compete with indigenous production. The word *maquila* also connotes for the Mexican people a certain proprietary aura over the means of production. The program has been carefully nurtured by the Mexican government since its inception in the 1960s and has become quite successful from the government's standpoint. It is now an important portion of the Mexican economy as a whole, involving thousands of factories and hundreds of thousands of workers.

What is the significance of the borderland between the United States and Mexico? Why do these factories fall into formation behind this imaginary line in the sand? A remote desert area, it is far from the economic and population centers of either country and devoid of the resources and infrastructure usually associated with industrial development. What sense does it make to ship components thousands of miles across the American West only to turn them around and ship them back in assembled form? What is it that is done to them on the other side of a border checkpoint that cannot be done in Ohio or California or Illinois? What is it that happens in Nogales, Sonora, that cannot happen two miles north in Nogales, Arizona?

The answer: subsistence employment and environmental pollution. These do not exist legally north of the border. American industrial producers can save money — a lot of money — avoiding union-scale wages and strict pollution laws by building factories south of the border.

The people who decide to assemble products in Mexico instead of the United States have no interest in dumping waste and exploiting Mexican peasants — all they want to do is save money. They *have* to save money. If they do not save money, companies in Japan, Europe, China, Korea, Thailand, and the Philippines will produce and sell the same products for less. Consumers will buy the foreign products instead of the American products. Even American consumers will buy the cheaper products from other countries. An American company pays a worker in Tijuana one-tenth of what it would pay in Pittsburgh and is able to wash its solvents down Tijuana's municipal drain or dumps them into its river. It does this not to be mean to the Mexican people but to stay in business. If it does the "right thing" — paying higher American wages and observing stricter American environmental laws — it will go out of business. In doing so, it will do no good for its workers, the environment, or consumers. When it goes out of business, companies in other countries will continue to produce in the cheapest way possible.

Many would say that maquiladoras are capital's way of getting around paying decent wages and that business owners use maquiladoras in their bargaining with labor to keep American wages down. This is true — but it is true because it *has* to be true. As long as market forces are allowed to direct the flow of goods and money, capital has to find the most cost-effective production process, and this translates to use of the cheapest reliable labor available. Businesses should not be expected to keep inefficient facilities in operation for the sake of social altruism: It's not what they are in business to do and certainly not what they do best. But businesses do not close factories because wages are high; they close them because wages are higher than somewhere else. It is not *absolutely* low wages that they look for — only *relatively* low wages. If all wages everywhere were $1 per hour — or even $100 per hour — there would be no incentive to shut down factories in one location and open them somewhere else. As markets continue to globalize, capital will continue to look for reliable workers, not with *low* wages but with the *lowest* wages in the world. That is where the jobs will go. As long as one country keeps strong legislation protecting its workers and another does not, the jobs will go to the country that does not. Maquiladoras will continue to drain jobs away from American workers for as long as Mexican workers are unprotected.

The single biggest cost component of industrial production is labor. Labor is much more expensive in America than in other countries, and American products are, because of this, at a great competitive disadvantage on the world market. American companies have to look for ways to keep labor costs in line with those of companies they compete with. This puts American workers in direct competition with very poor and often desperate people all over the world. Hungry peasants in China and Mexico are delighted to have jobs that self-respecting American workers would not begin to consider.

American workers and workers in other industrialized countries have organized themselves into trade unions and struggled for generations to achieve national legislation guaranteeing higher wages, the forty-hour work week, safe working conditions, and compensation for injuries suffered on the job. American workers are provided by law with a livable wage, comfort and safety on the job, and a degree of economic security in the events of unemployment, accident, and old age. These provisions give the working class the chance to participate in the prosperity they have done so much to create, and we have become used to them as part of the American tradition. Good labor legislation has eased class conflict in American society and remains an essential cornerstone of the American way of life. Working-class prosperity also contributes to prosperity in general by creating more paying customers for American business.

But many developing countries do not yet have good labor legislation. Some countries, like Mexico, have a minimum wage, workers compensation, social security, and severance pay, but these are slight by American standards and are unevenly enforced. For the most part, workers are still extremely poor but undemanding. Unions are weak and often represent the interests of government or industry as much as those of workers themselves. Maquila factories in Mexico are a growing threat to the American way of life because they allow American companies to compete in the world market by circumventing American labor legislation. The line in the sand between Mexico and the United States has become a line between good and bad national labor legislation. American-owned factories spring up along it, their front doors open to the coming and going of American goods and their back doors open to Mexican workers.

The Mexican government is so pleased to have the employment, the hard currency, and the value-added taxes provided by maquiladoras that they have done little to protect Mexican workers. The Mexican government knows that it must keep wages low to keep the system going and has gone out of its way to do so in order to keep American business interested in the maquila program. Minimum wages are fifteen to twenty percent of what they are in America, and they do not keep up with inflation.

What is even harder on workers is the government's consistent pattern of devaluating the peso. A less-valuable peso means that payroll dollars from across the border go much farther, and actual labor costs become lower still. But because maquila "boom towns" just south of the border did not yet have adequate retail outlets and other services, Mexican workers were in the habit of buying many of their groceries and other necessities with dollars on the American side of the border. The peso became so devalued in the 1970s and 1980s as to make it virtually worthless against the dollar, forcing workers to buy lower-quality goods on their own side of the border at inflated prices.

The Mexican government has also relaxed labor laws and their enforcement. In the early days of the maquila program, there were laws on the books requiring severance pay for layoffs, but layoffs without pay have since become routine. There is now an acceptable ninety-day "probationary period" where new workers can be hired below minimum wage, and social security fund payment requirements by employers have been reduced.[7] The Mexican–American border's significance to the program is that labor laws are good to the north of it and bad to the south of it, and this keeps business hopping to the south.

Another factor that keeps business hopping south of the border is lax environmental legislation and enforcement. By moving to Mexico, many companies get away with levels of air, water, and soil pollution that would be impossible in the U.S. The New River, which flows through a concentration of maquiladora factories in Mexicali and then north into the U.S., was used for years as drainage for millions of gallons of raw sewage and industrial waste. It was declared by the U.S. Geological Survey, the state of California, and the Imperial County Health Department to be the "dirtiest river in America."[8] Environmental conditions within factories are also less scrutinized by the Mexican government. A film-processing plant moved to Mexicali after being cited by the Office of Safety Hazard Administration for unsafe working conditions, and a department of GTE was moved from Albuquerque, New Mexico, to Juarez, Mexico, after sixty-four workers filed for compensation for chemical poisoning. Environmental conditions are generally improving in the maquiladoras, but they remain far behind those north of the border, and Maquila owners are hesitant to invest in environmentally friendly technologies where there is little political will to create and enforce environmental legislation. Mexican officials are generally afraid to increase enforcement for fear of driving up production costs for the American-owned industries they depend on.

The border is a division between good environmental laws and not-so-good environmental laws. As with labor, it is the *differential* and not the *absolute* that is and must be exploited by capital. If environmental laws and enforcement were uniform on both sides of the border, whether good or bad, the incentive to close factories in America and open them in Mexico would disappear. If labor laws and environmental laws were the same on both sides of the border, the maquiladoras would lose their purpose. With uniform environmental and labor laws, most Mexicans would be willing to work for less than most Americans for a long time to come, but they would have no unfair advantages in the market for factory labor. In time, a world standard of living would emerge from the current chaos and injustice of globalization, and all workers would be given the chance to compete on the basis of skill and competence rather than on willingness to accept bad working conditions and environmental degradation.

The maquiladora program is an example of globalization without globalism. Capital markets flourish in a divided world because they exploit the uneven playing field created by differences from nation to nation in labor and environmental legislation. Capital is relatively easy to move across international boundaries and has expanded to a global scale much sooner than awareness of labor and the environmental justice. Exporting *capital* can be as easy as putting a check in an envelope, but exporting *labor* means uprooting communities and dislocating lives. Capital does not depend on world political unity to do business, but it, too, will benefit in the long run from a more comprehensive international legal system. The current globalization of business is part of an overall trend toward world unity; however, the injustices and degradation left in its wake are not the result of a unified world economy but of a new world economy without world protection of working people and natural communities.

The world is too small and business too big to keep trade and capital behind national barriers. The international scale of business is here to stay, and doing away with abuses of maquila-style systems of production through national protectionism would be unwise and impractical. We are on the road to global free trade, and there is no way back. Neither should we expect the World Trade Organization (WTO) to protect workers and the environment: That is the role of government. By creating a new scale of international trade, the North American Free Trade Agreement (NAFTA), the General Agreement on Tariffs and Trade (GATT), and the WTO have created a new set of legal problems on the international level that they cannot handle by themselves. Maquiladoras are geographically in Mexico but economically within the United States. Mexico is essentially exporting labor, which is a new phenomenon in political and economic relations, and America is finding a lower international legal denominator on which to conduct business. These are problems that can be handled only by government on the international level and eventually only on the global level. Bilateral agreements between the U.S. and Mexico protecting workers and the environment could relieve maquiladora abuses along the common border, but the same abuses would likely end up being exported to other parts of the world. As we are now finding the world to be a closed biological system and a closed economic system, we will soon be finding it a single closed legal system as well.

Strong and effective global labor laws will take many years and perhaps generations to enact. There are too many desperate people looking for work for any American- or European-style system of worker protection to arise on the global level anytime soon. Uniform labor laws will require movement toward a world standard of living that is still a long way off. There will be global standards of production and consumption in time, but they will evolve slowly.

Far more quickly realized will be uniform environmental laws. There is no reason why a company or an individual should be allowed to pollute the air and the water in one nation and not in another. Differences in environmental legislation from nation to nation are incentives for international businesses to seek the lowest levels of protection and, thereby, incentives to pollute. Workers and the environment will be protected ultimately only by a united global government. This is a practical truth.

8. Geo-engineering

WE HAVE ALREADY ALTERED THE EARTH'S NATURAL SYSTEMS without intention; should we consider altering them on purpose? Should we attempt, for instance, to engineer the climate?

I do not know the answer to this question and will not attempt to answer it. What I will do is ask the question in a better way. How we ask it depends on who we think we are. If, on the one hand, we are prospectors looking for new sources of terrestrial wealth, the question becomes something like this: "Should we attempt to engineer the biosphere so as to improve it, or should we shape it to meet our needs? As we increase the scope and scale of our technical abilities, should we consider altering something as encompassing as the climate for our own benefit? Should we try to make the climate more comfortable or perhaps make it more conducive to agricultural or forest production?"

If, on the other hand, we are one of several life forces attempting to establish harmony within the biosphere, the question becomes "Should we consider altering a natural balance so as to correct an imbalance that we already created?" This is the better question but one that we should not pretend to ask, much less to answer, until we reach the level of self-awareness that it presupposes.

The question is a very dangerous one. If answered too soon or answered improperly, it could result in irreparable harm to our own lives and to life itself. We could get ourselves into something that we do not understand and that we cannot get back out of. "Improving" nature is a risky business; things easily could go wrong. But eventually the question will be asked. We are becoming so powerful a force on Earth that we will soon have to consider how to maintain natural balances that used to maintain themselves. The climate is a prime example.

The Kyoto Protocol does not regulate the atmosphere. It only attempts to reduce the level of human effect on the atmosphere. But emissions have been ongoing for centuries and will continue, even with Kyoto. Carbon levels will continue to rise no matter how stringently emissions are controlled: Humans cannot stop burning fuels altogether. All that can be done from the emissions side of the equation is to make the problem not as bad as if nothing were done. We can reduce the rate at which we continue to damage the atmosphere. The problem may be limited this way, but it will not be fixed, or even kept from getting worse. Something like Kyoto may have to do for the time being, but it will not be good enough by the middle and late twenty-first century when serious climate change symptoms are likely to occur.

The other side of the carbon equation is the creation of carbon "sinks," or storage systems that tie up carbon in the form of biomass or limestone. A forest, an acre of phytoplankton, or any living system is a carbon sink in that it removes carbon dioxide from the air through photosynthesis and turns it into carbohydrate. Calcium carbonate, or limestone, is also a deposit of living systems that removes dissolved CO_2 from water, which can keep it from getting back into the air.

But carbon sinks are in retreat everywhere in the world. Tropical forests are disappearing by the millions of acres, and limestone coral reefs are dying off in the oceans. Even phytoplankton is in decline. Efforts were made at Kyoto to encourage governments to form new carbon sinks by allowing the carbon they remove from the air to offset emissions allotments, but the difference in the overall equation will not be much. There are some areas of the world where reforestation may make a difference, but it is unlikely to offset more than a small part of ongoing deforestation.

In any case, *reforestation* does not constitute *geo-engineering* in that reforestation merely puts back what was once there; climatic geo-engineering would mean creating enough new carbon-absorbing biomass to actually reduce the overall level of carbon in the air. This would mean growing biomass on a massive scale where it never existed before. There is not much land available for this. Already there is enormous pressure on existing forest and agricultural lands and little likelihood of finding substantial acreage for additional biomass production. But land covers only about a quarter of the earth's surface. Large-scale biomass geo-engineering will have to occur somewhere on the other three quarters.

Water covers about seventy-two percent of the earth's surface. More photosynthesis occurs in the oceans than on land, but the biomass produced is relatively small. Phytoplankton does not tie up nearly as much carbon per square foot of terrestrial surface as do trees. But you cannot grow trees in the ocean — at least, not yet. If a way could be found to do so on a massive scale, photosynthesis on the surface of the oceans could be used to tie up enormous amounts of carbon from the atmosphere.

One way of doing this would be to construct thousands of large concrete barges, fill them with manufactured soil, and plant them with trees. Enough floating tree farms could engineer a climatic balance by altering the carbon cycle just enough to restore a pre-industrial atmosphere. CO_2 removed from the atmosphere would become wood fiber. The trees would be used for lumber and help relieve pressure on natural land-based forests.

Each tree, of course, would be temporary, but the sink would be permanent. As trees were harvested and used for lumber, their carbon content would in time return to the atmosphere, but new trees would be planted in their place. Total biomass would remain at whatever level proved necessary. Forage and row crops grown on floating platforms could produce additional biomass and would provide an expanded food supply. Floating farms could also be used for renewable fuel production. As fossil fuels begin to run out, renewable carbon fuels could be produced over the oceans that could be consumed in accordance with need to balance atmospheric carbon levels.

The problem we are currently having with the earth's climate is that we are gradually restoring an atmosphere that existed hundreds of millions of years ago, during the early Carboniferous Era. The greenhouse effect was in full swing at the time: There was much more CO_2 in the air than there is now, and the climate was hotter and stormier. Plant life thrived in the warm, humid, carbon-rich environment. The more comfortable climate we enjoy today was created as vast quantities of carbon were removed from the air when carbon-based plant material became trapped under-water, forming oil, gas, and coal deposits. These "fossil fuels" became a vast carbon sink, as the CO_2 removed by the plants was unable to return to the air. But as we burn fossil fuels today, we return the same carbon to the atmosphere and restore some-thing like the hotter, stormier early Carboniferous climate. Engineering a massive artificial carbon sink on the surface of the oceans could be an attempt to replace the carbon sinks destroyed as fossil fuel deposits are burned. The difference would be that where the energy we now get from fossil fuels originated in the solar radiation of hundreds of millions of years ago, the energy and fiber we might use from artificial biomass production would be from current solar energy. Because it would be from incoming present-day sunlight, we would be in a position to create a renewable fiber and energy supply and at the same time control the carbon content of the atmosphere. If the CO_2 level is too high, we will grow more biomass. If it gets too low (as when we stop burning fossil fuels) we may have to grow less biomass fuel and instead burn more.[9]

But I do not suggest that creating artificial biomass is an an-swer because there is no way to know if it is technically feasible or that it would not create more problems than it solves. Covering vast areas of the ocean's surface would rob marine life of photosynthesis, reduce photoplankton, and affect whatever natural systems depend on it. It would also reduce water temperatures and disturb ocean currents. The construction of huge numbers of floating platforms for tree and crop production would have untold environmental consequences. The production of concrete from limestone (calcium carbonate) releases carbon dioxide into the atmosphere. If concrete were used to build the rafts, enormous amounts of carbon would be released in that process. Ironically, the problem might get much worse in the process of getting better.

There is simply no way to engage in so massive a project without huge environmental effects. And even if it could be accomplished within acceptable levels of ecological dislocation, there is still no way to know if it would work. It could go horribly wrong, and we could throw the entire biosphere out of some balance that we do not even know exists. We have never had the chance to play around with a climate before, and we will not get a second chance.

Geo-engineering on this scale would also produce a whole new dynamic to the human community. If we become able to affect the climate, even marginally, we become responsible for it. If there are storms or droughts or it is too hot or too cold, there will be someone to blame it on. Whatever political mechanism is developed to regulate atmospheric carbon levels may be perceived as *in control* of how things are going. The weather might be perceived to be like the economy — something the government makes happen. Governments have less control over employment and inflation than people think, but they become responsible for economic activity because of the marginal effects they do have. Governments become responsible for the economy because they have some control over interest rates, spending, currency, and taxes. Whatever policy board decides to plant more trees or release more fuel may have to answer for droughts and hurricanes.

We may one day have to pick leaders with the best *weather policy*.

In any case, I do not believe that humanity has the spiritual maturity at this point to begin any sort of geo-engineering. It is too big a step. It would be asserting our legitimacy as one of — and at one with — the major elemental forces in the terrestrial system. We are not ready yet because we are only beginning to learn the difference between control and balance. Oceanic bio-mass engineering would be creating Earth at the expense of Water to restore balance between Air and Energy, and we do not yet understand what that means. It is out of our league for now.

But the question of geo-engineering will arise. We will be in a position to consider it when we are no longer politically divided and our attention and resources are no longer diverted to protecting ourselves from one another. We will be able to answer it when there is the possibility for a general consensus among all the earth's people that it is the right thing to do.

Part III — The Spiritual

9. Spiritual Humanism

THERE IS A PLACE TO KNOW THE UNITY OF ALL PEOPLE.

It is deeper than everyday appearances, more compelling than intellectual realization, more profoundly moving than the promise of practical survival. It is not merely known but felt, now and everyday. It is always there — you may see it now — but you will not see it until you look.

Forget, for now, the reasons for world unity. Forget the politics and wars and oceans and satellite technologies. Look at what makes you and me *human*. It cannot be language, for language is specific to nationality, and nationality is what we are trying to move past. Look past language and see what there is that is human. See what you actually experience *now*. There is the feeling of the body: the arms and legs and shoulders and neck. Feel each of them. Feel the feet against the floor and the back on the chair. Feel the bones inside the muscles. Feel tendons gliding over joints. This is *being*, but it is not distinctly human; you share what you feel with animals and trees and the rocks and soils of the earth. It is *being*, but not *human being*. Little of what you are is uniquely human.

Feel now the breath moving in and out of your body. Feel the lungs filling and the rise and fall of the diaphragm. Feel the atmosphere. This is your relation to every living thing on Earth. Air is a great sharing, and it is your connection to every plant and animal. Plants breathe in as you breathe out and out as you in. They push; you pull. Yang and yin. They give you the life you return to them. Breath is everything living but not specially human. Little of your being is distinctly human.

Next, feel the heartbeat; feel the blood coursing through your veins. Watch the pulse and throb of fluid through your arms and neck; hear the rhythm of animal motion pushing through your body, giving the gift of mobility. This is your connection to the oceans and to the enclosed ocean of animal being. This is the piece of you that you share with the birds and the fish and the beasts of the field. This is you the animal but not you the human. So much of you is rocks and plants and animals. But what is distinctly human?

Look now at the flame of thought that burns through what you feel and see and sense. Watch thoughts rising and falling, twisting through the background of sensation and perception. This is humanity. Not *your* humanity — humanity. It is not yet yours. Do not wait until it has become you. Do not let it form distinct concepts and words, for this will be the gravity of self and nationality that shapes and twists thought into what you call reality. Do not let it, for now, shape what you are looking at.

Later, it will return, and with it will come what you call reality. It will tell you what reality is and include itself, but look past it for now. Look down into consciousness below the place where thoughts become language. This is humanity. This is you, as a human. It is a small part of you, for you are also breath and rock and ocean. It is only here that you may see humanity in relation to wind and rocks and oceans. You share it with all people.

We are ideation before it becomes words, symbols emerging in the mind that represent experience but are not yet sensation and are not yet associated with a particular sound: language that is not yet words. It is at this point that we emerge from the plants and birds and trees, as humans, but before we are any type of human. It is where we begin to think but before we think anything in particular. It is the unity of all people.

The chatter of thought is not distinct and geometric like objects seen and touched in perceptual reality. Thoughts come and go, appearing and disappearing before we are aware of them. Once gone, they never return. They do not hold still and let us touch them; they are not stationary in time. Time is, perhaps, stationary in them. They boil and tumble through the mind without apparent order or meaning. It is we who give them order and meaning. We draw from them like a dipper from a pool, containing them in the vessel of self as they pass in and out of being. Through self, and the larger self of nationality, we shape thought into what makes sense to us. We develop distinct concepts of place and geography, history and culture, home and work. When unaware of thought, thinking stops, leaving the concepts to shape what we think. We make the world and live in it. This is sanity and practical living on the operational level; there is no other way to get through the day.

Humanity is fundamentally without form and without substance, as we have found it here. There are thoughts of what it means to be human in the non-national sense, but these are weak and undeveloped. They do not cause us to act. Humanity is fluid and chaotic. There is not enough structure to develop a course of action. To become a humanity that does things — that takes care of the oceans and the air and of itself — concepts will have to arise from thought and become words — words that we do not now speak.

From the words will develop a sense of *self* that can *do*. But the self will never be fully defined. We will never be entirely sure who we are. There will be no others that we are not. There will be no background against which to appear better, stronger, or more moral. There will be no luxury of rebounding ourselves off of that which we are not. There will be no examples to avoid: no walls — only mirrors. Concepts of humanity will rise from thought and take shape but also remain fluid, verging on the chaotic. They will never be as plain and straightforward as flags and anthems and cartographic shapes. They will never be as easy to point to. This is within keeping of the fundamental nature of human substance. It is the chatter of the mind.

It will come to the surface when we need to know what to do with our Earth, and from it will come a sort of policy. We will know ourselves in relation to rocks and water, and we will know how much we may safely take and how much to leave. We will know how to deal with quarrels among our own kind, for that is what the chatter is. We will listen to the chatter, stand back from it, and watch it take form and become us. We will listen to it arise and enter into what we have listened to before. We will watch it do battle with itself. This is the spirit of humanity.

It is a deep place, a quiet place despite the chatter and remote from everyday life. But it is in and around everyday life. It is not the final ground of being or the ultimate reality. It is as deep as you can go and still be you, but it is not as deep as there is. Humanity is not the whole of being. Nor is it the center of being, except as we see it.

You cannot say that you were there. You cannot say or do anything nonhuman, though you may have experienced it. Being nonhuman is the way to understand being human, but what you say will be through the agency of your humanity. Language and symbol separate you as you say or think. There can be no saying and no expectation of doing beyond language.

But when you have seen, come and look again at humanity — where the action is. Come and see what can be done. This is where life most needs awareness of itself in evolutionary process. Go to that place to see the wholeness of humanity, and come here to see what most needs doing.

Human consciousness is changing rapidly. It will not long be what we think it is now. We know from historical records that it has evolved rapidly to the present. Record keeping is a recent development, beginning only in the last 5,500 years — less than one percent of human existence. Within that short time, the human mind has become something enormously different.

To know humanity, look at the Fire of thought. To know the wholeness of humanity, look past the Fire to the Water below, where there is no humanity. This cannot be done; it must be waited for. There is no vessel there, no container for the primordial waters of being, no means to draw from the deep, and nothing to bring back with you. You must drink it there. It will fill you in and out, and there will be no thing that is or is not you. As you return, the waters will take the form of the vessel you give them. You will see humanity in its wholeness and rebecome nearly what you were.

10. Texas and the Holy Spirit

IF IT IS GOOD TO BE CHRISTIAN AND AMERICAN, IT MAY NOT be good to be something else. It may be evil. It is unwise, therefore, to change being within the realm of ideas. It is better to look for what is right beyond what is thought to be right.

Outside Hamburger Rock, the desert wind wailed for several days. A thin red dust covered the windward folds of the tent and coated the camp stove left outside to cool overnight. I looked out through the flap, hoping for a day calm enough to walk through. I wanted to get out of the tent and into the sands and mesas and dry riverbeds that stretched for hundreds of miles around me, and this would be the day. Before the winds had me campbound, I had been east up Hart's Draw and south toward Six-Shooter Peak, the Colorado River to the west. The sun was gaining a foothold in the blue September sky, and the day was warming. A single raven paddled through the air overhead. I had seen no one for nearly a week.

As I blew dust off the stove and pumped it up for morning coffee, I heard a vehicle on the paved road a mile or so to the south. A minute later I heard it slow and turn onto the dirt road that came toward where I stood. I lit the stove, put a pot of water on to boil, and looked up toward the road. The sound became three vehicles, then four, two of them pulling large white-paneled trailers. Dust streamed out behind them. As they reached a curve in the road that led down to Indian Creek Canyon, they stopped, as if deciding which way to go, and then slowly, one by one, turned off the dirt road and drove across the desert floor toward the rock formation that was my temporary home. This can't be good, I thought, as they filed by and stopped a short distance away. A red, white, and blue sticker on a rear window said "Standing Tall." I waved, halfheartedly, and they waved back.

Men in jeans and cowboy hats piled out of pickup trucks and began sorting through tools and pieces of equipment. Trailer doors opened, all-terrain vehicles rolled down ramps, and gasoline cans passed hand to hand. Voices cracked the still morning air, and engines began to roar. Before long, a half dozen buggies fanned out across the desert floor, bumping over rocks and gullies and cryptobiotic soils. Dust plumes piled, billowed, and settled back to earth as the snarl of spark plugs and pistons trailed off in the distance. My world was utterly violated. Soon all was quiet again. The desert is so vast here it absorbs us, even us.

My day was ruined — or at least diverted. I no longer felt like walking to the Colorado River. Instead, I sat in the folding chair for hours, as I had been sitting for days. The sun climbed high over Lookout Point, and I scanned the horizon. When it became too hot in the sun, I moved to the shade in the rock crevice next to my parked car, plugged the laptop computer in to the inverter, and began writing. I wrote and wrote, as I had been hoping I would do, and forgot about the sun, and the dust, and the mesas in the distance. I wrote about deserts and rocks and places I had been, and I wrote and wrote until the battery went dead and it was dark.

They were back, I knew, because I could hear their words in the night, and the low rumble of their laughter. But I slept that night — slept well. I awoke before dawn and stood for an hour outside my tent, watching the dark hills turn red and brown in early daylight. They awoke after the chill had burned off and began puttering around vehicles and camp stoves. After a meal and what sounded to me like a second cup of coffee, I headed toward their campsite, hoping to catch them before they left. I didn't have to start the car today, I told myself, but until I did I was stuck here. What kind of idiot, I thought of them thinking as I walked within their view, would be out here without so much as a jumper cable?

"Hey," I heard, and said. No warmth, no smiles. I tried to think of something to say about the day, the dust, the chill, and internal combustion engines. Mostly there was "Yeah" and "Guess so" to what I came up with. They had gotten lost and separated the day before but found their way out just before dark. Some were going out on the desert again today, others heading back to town. Yeah, they could help me jump my car. "Need a ride back over there?"

Two men in a crew cab diesel showed up a few minutes later. Both were pot-bellied and unshaven and had revolvers strapped to their legs. Fortunately, when I had made camp I backed up to the rock crevice, leaving the hood end of the car safely accessible and the rear bumper sticker safely hidden. I popped the hood and gunned the engine as the clamp came down on the battery terminal. "What do I owe ya?" "No problem. Battery old?" "No, just ran it down — computer." "Huh." "Thanks — I would have been stuck here." "No problem, a man's gotta...."

Two weeks later I was driving across west Texas, looking for a radio station. The war was still playing itself out in its slow, dribbling way, and I hadn't heard anything. I was down on the low end of the dial, looking for an NPR station, and it wasn't there. No Carl Kasell, no Morning Edition, no kind of news I wanted to hear. I thought it would be everywhere, and it wasn't. I thought for sure I could get it on the interstate, but all I got was gospel, country and western, and not a little bit of fire and brimstone. I heard about America and families and the "Judeo-Christian tradition" and the perils of homosexuality and "neo-pagan relativism." What was I doing looking for NPR in west Texas? And why be in west Texas if you want to listen to NPR? What is the point of traveling a thousand miles from home if you're still in the bubble? So I listened to the gospel, and to the country and western, and to the fire and brimstone.

One singer said, "I might be a bad boy, but I'm a real good man." Another claimed he knew the "truth about men: we like to scratch and spit and cuss." Another was happy to be "a simple man: got my job and a piece of land." Others said, "I love this bar," or "That ain't my truck in her drive." I was touched by one about a little girl who asked her daddy if, when she died, could she "see grandpa," "taste the Milky Way," and "help God pour out the rain?" It was simple, beautiful, and utterly complete. Why not? And then there was "Have you forgotten nine-eleven? Some people say this country's just lookin' for a fight. I'd say they're right."

This was Texas, but not only Texas: It was America. And not only America: This was the part of America driving the rest of America into the rest of the world. This was the spirit, alive and strong and well, that makes this country what it is, standing tall in a world that needed to be shown a thing or two. These were men — good, honest men — who believed in God and heaven and doing what's right. They believed in doing what needed to be done and in getting even. The time for talk was over. We've had our Pearl Harbor — now let's roll!

I listened all day long, into central Texas and east Texas. The spirit crept in through my boots and jeans, and I wanted a hat — maybe not a cowboy hat — but something with a little more character than the old baseball cap on my head. By the end of the day I loved these guys and wanted to be one of them. I wanted to stop in a bar, order a beer, smoke a Marlboro. These were my people. We believe in God and America, and when they attack us, we fight back. We will do what any fool can see needs doing. They, whoever they are, killed thousands of our people — can there be greater clarity than that?

The Holy Spirit is fellowship. When It is present, you see It. You see It in the tears and laughter of people. You do not have to believe it to see It. Of the three persons of the Trinity, It is the one you can see in this world now.

When you are with people you know and love, It is there. It is not the people; It is the Spirit among the people. It is not human — not a he or a she or a father or son or mother. It is what you feel when you are with others who feel It. It is fellowship at a party, at the office, church, bar, funeral, or ball game. It is a joy in the life and goodness of those around you. It is your work unit, the team you are on, your congregation, the circle of your friends. It is the spirit of friendship and community. You see It now, in this life, but It is not of the earth.

Fellowship is the celebration of being human. It does not matter what type of human; it is ourselves allowing ourselves to be as we are, no matter what we are. It is laughter with friends at the silliness of being human. The Holy Spirit allows weakness — loves it, even — and it becomes funny. The Holy Spirit will never deny Itself. It will never deny the humanity It celebrates. The deepest laughter is at ourselves being less than we think we are.

But fellowship extends to all people. In another country or another neighborhood, with the friends of your children or the friends of people you do not know, there is fellowship. There is a sameness in the difference. The languages will not be the same and the jokes will not be the same, but there will be fellowship. You smile at the waiter, talk to the cabdriver, give a dollar to the old woman in the street. This is the Holy Spirit. It is not noisy or obnoxious. Often silent, It may not smile or wish you a nice day. It may wait. Laughing with friends, It flows naturally and easily; with your enemies It is slow and awkward and joy itself. Laughing with enemies is joy itself. Do this with great care.

The Holy Spirit arises from deep in the human soul, down below language and race and gender, but this is only an idea. I think it is true — I want it to be true — but I know that it is only an idea. I know the Holy Spirit is among those who celebrate themselves apart from others and from me. It is with the enemy. I can see It even in him.

I cannot be a cowboy because a cowboy needs an Indian, and I do not see one. The Holy Spirit has placed him on a reservation, but I will look even there. I will look, and when I find him I will speak in whatever language seems appropriate or in no language at all, and I will say something about the day. And when I have said it, I will look the Holy Spirit in the eye of the face It does not have and send It away. I will wait, saying nothing, until It returns.

11. Omi O Lota

I WAS ON THE SHORE OF THE ATLANTIC OCEAN IN CAPE Coast, Ghana.

Oscar, a Cuban with thin lips and light brown skin, looked almost as out-of-place as I did. He was proud of his island nation. "What are the two things you worry about most?" he asked. "Education and health care. We have them both, for free. It is not a wealthy country, and I cannot support everything that has happened, but these two things are free." He had been in West Africa for two years. He knew very little English, and no Fanti at all, and I could not imagine how he managed to live and work. "Castro is not the saint some say he is, but he is not what you say he is, either."

"I did not say he was anything."

"But you have been trying to choke us for forty years." I was not quick to pick up the subtleties of the second-person form. "I don't see why you have to interfere with a different way of doing things, as if we are a threat to you. We are a threat only if there is some truth in what we are trying to do. What are you afraid of?"

He had approached our table in the far corner of the open-air bar after exchanging a word with several others in the crowd. Kayode and I had noticed him earlier from across the room and traded quiet suggestions as to where he might be from. In America, he would have been considered black; in Africa he was clearly white. Kayode thought him European, perhaps Spanish or Portuguese; I thought mixed Hispanic or maybe Pacific Islander.

Kayode, a Nigerian, spoke no Spanish and did not understand what we were saying but had heard him mention Sango and wanted to know how Sango had crossed the ocean. The sun had set over the beach toward El Mina an hour or so before, and the night was cool and quiet. People were still jumping in the surf and playing on the beach below where we sat. A half moon arced high overhead, and waves were breaking on the rocks.

"I think you have some good things going. Everyone would like to have education and health care regardless of income — and guaranteed employment, too. There should be a way of doing this without eliminating individual initiative and market forces — certainly without eliminating democracy. I am very interested in this sort of thing. But in your case, it has become entangled in geopolitics."

"Why? Why can't you accept another way of doing things? If not for yourselves, why not for us? Why do you treat us like criminals for doing things our own way? Why do you want everybody else in the world to do things your way?"

"It seems the world can have only one idea at a time or, at least, one nuclear-tipped idea."

"You would have crushed us."

"We nearly crushed ourselves."

Oscar repeated some of what he said in broken English, but Kayode was not following it.

"Ask him," Kayode said, "if Sango is still the lightning and thunder."

"Yes, he is," Oscar assured. "And he speaks with fire. Fire comes from his mouth when he is angry. He is very powerful and people fear him. He pleats his hair as a woman."

Kayode smiled. "He learned this from Oya, who does the same. He liked how it looked on her and asked her to do it for him." Kayode was pleased to see that Sango lived on in the New World. He knew from the African–Americans he had met that Yoruba culture and religion were experiencing a revival in the

U.S., but here was someone who had direct experience with Sango. Here was someone who knew Sango the way he did.

"And he is a man for six months of the year, and a woman for the other six," added Oscar.

Kayode's face dropped. His eyes shifted, and he looked at me uneasily. The wind was picking up and a large wave crashed on the beach below where we sat. I was looking over the railing at the fortress a hundred yards down the beach to the east, where slaves had been held for deportation. A stark and distinctly non-African-looking structure, it was built by the British to counter-point the Portuguese (later Dutch) fortress at El Mina, barely visible on the horizon to the west. Both castles had served as gathering points for human cargo on its way across the Atlantic. A long row of heavy black iron cannon pierced the thick stone walls and shone in the moonlight.

"I don't know where he got that from," Kayode said to me. "It is not exactly Yoruba."

Earlier in the day Kayode and I had gone to the British fortress and visited the dungeon where slaves had awaited shipment to the Caribbean and North America. I sat on the floor with my back against the wall, trying to imagine people lying on the stone floor next to me, waiting. They waited and waited, but did not know what they were waiting for. They did not know where they were or where they were going. They did not know where their wives and parents and children were or if any of them had survived the raids. No one they loved would ever know what was happening to them. Most were from the forestlands farther north and had never seen the ocean. They did not know what the ocean was. They did not know how to swim, or what swimming was. I closed my eyes to the light and saw what was real. There were shouts echoing from the walls and filth on the floor. Someone was shouting, but I could not hear what was said. The air smelled of naked bodies, excrement, and rotting food. I turned on the floor and felt a stone against my hip. Someone — I did not know who

— *had felt it there before. Someone had been here and was now gone. I felt the illness of heart — and the waiting — and I felt the never-ending fear that the waiting would end. My body ached. It pulled on me, pulling me away from the room and the people around me, away from the sky and the trees and people that I always knew. I felt the muscles and bones of my body leaving who I was, as if they would no longer be who I was. I did not want to live like this. I was sick in my heart and I did not want to live, but someone was coming and I had to stand. I did not want to stand and would not have to stand if I could stop living right here, right now. But there would be pain, pain worse than not living. Pain would be there to keep me alive, and I would live for its sake. I cried, but there were no tears. Muscles in my legs and arms were tightening, and I felt my feet draw up beneath my body. Light appeared at the edge of my eyes, and I stood. I could go now. It was time to leave, and I could go now.* Kayode was whispering a Yoruba prayer at the Door of No Return.

"Sango and Osun are still very strong in Cuba," Oscar was saying. "You call it voodoo in the U.S."

"You should come to the Sacred Grove in Oshogbo and to Ile-Ife," said Kayode. "You should learn about Sango and Osun." Oscar nodded, but he will not go.

I am in the Sacred Grove on the banks of the Osun River. There is a circle around me, and I am lying on the ground. To the north is Air and Night, Death, Winter, and the nonbeing of things. It is the arctic and high mountains. To the east is Earth, Morning, Birth, Spring, and the beginning of things: the forest with its animals and lush plant life. Kayode's hands are in the river, and he is giving thanks for the water, for fertility, and for protection, guidance, and good fortune. He is asking for me. A large fish is swimming in the pool in front of us. He comes to the surface and I hear a strong sucking sound as he curves and twists his long body then dives below. I do not see him. Birds

are in the trees overhead, and I hear the water rippling over rocks.
Kayode will watch for me.

He told the story of Osun to Anjili, who was not impressed.
Anjili is a Burba from Maiduguri, in far northeastern Nigeria, highly
educated, and skeptical of traditional religions. He listened, but
he had heard it before. Long, long ago, before the coming of the
Portuguese, the people of Oshogbo lived in peace and prosperity
along the banks of the Osun. They drank her water, washed and
bathed along her banks, and carried water to the sprouting yams
and alligator peppers. There was enough land for everyone and
plenty to eat. Woven cloth, beads, and iron tools were available
in the marketplace on the hill above the river. The people gave
thanks to Osun, who had lain on the ground and become their
river. The people felt the flow of the river through their crops and
through their bodies and through their children and were thankful
for what they had. They were healthy, there was peace in the
land, and the people were happy.

But one day the Babalawo had a great vision and came to the
priestess, the Iya-orisa, and told her that there was danger on the
other side of the river. The people of Ijeshi coveted the lands and
the people of Oshogbo and were preparing an invasion. The
fields would be taken, the men enslaved, and the women made
wives of Ijeshi men. The people were afraid and prepared to flee
into the forest. But the Babalawo said that the people should not
run away. Instead, they should light the sixteen fires of the sacred
lamp and prepare a sacrifice to Osun. He did not know how
Osun would protect them, but he assured them that she would.
A calabash was to be prepared with offerings of orogbo (bitter
kola), obi (kola nuts), and atare (alligator pepper), and the calabash carried to the banks of the river on the head of a virgin.
Trusting in Osun and the Babalawo, the Iya-orisa instructed the
people to stay in the village and to select a virgin from their midst.
This they did and prepared the sacrifice. The next day the virgin
walked from the village through the Sacred Grove with the

calabash on her head. When she came to the river, she opened the calabash and cast the offering to Osun. That night, as the warriors of Ijeshi prepared to attack, the river rose and spread out across the forest so that they could not cross.

Anjili smiled. "It was a coincidence. They could not make the river flood by throwing things into it. Rivers flood all the time."

Kayode continued. The miracle of Osun was not what she did for Oshogbo but what she did for the Ijeshi. The day after the planned attack the waters subsided and the river returned to its banks. The Ijeshi came back to the river but did not cross to attack Oshogbo. Impressed with the power of Osun to bring peace to the peoples of Yorubaland and the ability of Oshogbo to protect itself without war, they resolved to live in peace with the peoples on the other side of the river. They would reject the reasons for war that had seemed so important the day before. They crossed the river that day not with spears and knives but with gifts of food and jewelry and owo eyo (cowries shells) and negotiated a lasting peace with Oshogbo. They brought peace with them instead of taking it away. From that day to this, the people of Oshogbo celebrate the peace of Osun with a procession every August through the Sacred Grove to the banks of the river. The Iya-orisa selects a virgin, and the people follow her as she carries the calabash on her head and offers the sacrifice to Osun. The power of Osun is so well known and respected throughout Yorubaland that since the spreading of the waters on that night hundreds of years ago, no one has dared attack Oshogbo.

Anjili rolls his eyes. "It's a nice story."

To the south is Fire, Youth, Midday, and the middle of things. It is the desert and Summer. To the west is Rain, Evening, Old Age, Autumn, and the end of things. It is the ocean. I am in the circle still, in the Sacred Grove, in the land between the earth and the Sky, on the banks of the Nolin River, flowing toward the ocean. I am in the river. The Owl has become the Fish and swims down over the rocks and through the pale waters to the mouth of the

river. We swim as one. In the ocean it is night and clear — a bright
moon washes the black sky. The water is cold and the distance is
great. We swim on. Off the coast of Africa, we enter the river and
swim against the current. But I am not Yoruba and do not know
the ways of Osun. I do not know the Babalawo and the Orisas. It
is upstream and no longer where the waters blend and do not
flow. They flow past me easily on all sides, but I cannot stop to
rest. I am not at ease. I push on, bend after bend, over the rocks
and through pools and on to the Sacred Grove. There are birds in
the trees overhead. Osun is here. She is here and speaks to me.

I ask, "Who will take care of this place?"

"Do not worry about that," she says. My mouth opens and
she enters.

Kayode fills a bottle with water, giving thanks. "Oshea," he
says "Oshea."

We turn and drift with the river back toward the ocean, back
over rocks and around the bends. The earthen banks of Oshogbo
are on either side, containing the waters. Villagers are on the
banks, hoeing their gardens. There are children playing, and it is
hot. We swim past, down through the current, through the villages of Yorubaland to the ocean, where the banks disappear and
the waters mix. In the ocean, the waters of Osun mix with the
waters of every land.

"Reasons for peace are like reasons for war," she says. "Peace
is not something you make. It is what the fish swim through and
the animals breathe. It is everywhere and we are in it. Water has
no enemy."

"But it is here that the water will one day rise. It is here that
the reasons given for war will dissolve into nothing."

"Is that what you will say?"

"I don't know. What should I say?"

"Say what you will, but do not come here to find things to
say."

"The waters will rise, and nation will no longer rise against nation. That is what I will say."

"I am the mother of my people. I bring them children and the swelling of the yam root. I nourish them, as a mother nourishes and protects. It is the waters they remember. It is the waters they point to and remember. That is what you have seen."

"But why are you here now?"

"It is I who have found you."

"You will speak?"

"No! You are the one with the words and reasons and concepts to please your friends. Do not presume to extract from what you see here! The peace you speak of has no meaning without war. Without war it is nothing. Is that what you want? Nothing?"

She is angry with me, and I feel foolish and presumptive. But she smiles, and I know the waters will rise. I do not know why, but I know the waters will rise between the continents.

Long, long ago, before the coming of the Portuguese and the British, a baby girl opened her eyes on the marketplace. Strapped to her mother's back, she saw the bright colors of blankets spread on the ground, covered with cassava, yams, kola nuts, and cowries. She heard drumming and saw people dancing in the clearing on the top of the hill. Her little heart pounded with excitement as her mother's head turned to look for a place on the ground.

Years later, the girl returned to the marketplace carrying a basket of pounded yam on her head. Turning down the first offer, she moved through the crowd looking for eggs and dried fish. She found a place on the ground and began talking to the older women around her. She traded the yam with them for the things her mother wanted.

She returned many times after that and became known for her honesty and fairness in barter. Her trading was always beneficial for both sides, and many sought her out. As she grew to woman-hood, her mother and grandmother taught her the plants and herbs of the forest and the healing ways of the Oshogbo people. Leaving the gardening and weaving to others, she spent her days searching for plants in the forest and preparing medicines to trade in the marketplace. Through her grandmother she was initiated and became an Iya-orisa. People would come from surrounding villages to find her in the marketplace and ask for her advice on illnesses and family problems. Her reputation spread, and soon the king of Oyo learned of her powers. He sent for her advice several times. One day, he appeared in person and asked her to marry him. She agreed and left the village to live in the king's palace, but she would often disappear into the forest for days at a time.

Some say that she was never really a girl or a woman and would take on human form only when she returned to live with the King. One day, after the King sent her away, she lay on the ground and became the river that flows through the people of Oshogbo.

"What is my sacrifice?" I ask. "What is it I must do, or give up, in order to have peace?" We are in the ocean, it is dark, and the waters are not moving.

She says that there is no single answer. It is what it is and that is all. What you give up for peace is what your sacrifice will be. "What are the reasons for war?" she asks. "That is your sacrifice."

But I have no reasons for war.

"Then it will be something you think," she says. "If it is some-thing you want to give up, it will not be a sacrifice."

We are at the mouth of the Nolin River now, and we swim up through the current to where I live. Osun is in America. She will remain until my sacrifice is made, and I do not know what it is. No one has told me this. When it is made, I will pour the bottle into the river. She will be in the Sacred Grove when the festival comes.

12. Chesler Park

WHY THESE PARTICULAR SHAPES OF SANDSTONE? LAID DOWN under seawater, here these millions of years, now eroded to lumps and pillars and smooth blocks of red-brown and white: Why these shapes now? Why is there level parkland between the hoodoos? It is accidental, I am sure, by any mechanical understanding of geology and physical process — but why the beauty? If these were alive, we would say there is survival value in their beauty. That would explain it for us. But they are not alive — they are not evolving — they are eroding, devolving. But why so enormously beautiful? Why am I silent before them?

I have come to think of these strange forms as words of God. Words that I listen for as I look at them. They have been here for so many days of sun and moonless night, through so many winds and storms and tremors of the earth, these piers and pillars of Permian sediment. They might have worn evenly and smoothly and said something quite different. But they say what has been, and is. They do not speak of man and his quarrels, they speak of Earth and Rain. They are the words of God spoken to the Air before there was language.

These words, spoken ten million years ago, before an idea of God, before there were words and ideas of rock, before the idea of time: Was there a god then who spoke them? Does His word erode to what I see now? What mind is it now that overlays these rocks with time? The shapes and colors before me, hidden within earlier words, now open to air and light: This is truth I listen to now, and what truth is. This is what God does.

Through His word we learn to live in community. He spoke; we listened, thinking in words, heard Him. We learned to love one another as ourselves. Muhammad, Moses, Jesus, Buddha, Lao-Tse, Confucius, Zoroaster, Mahavira: Each taught us to live greater lives through each other than through ourselves. God taught us then what we could know.

He speaks even now. He did not stop speaking one thousand or two thousand years ago. To listen one must look: God speaks even now with great power and awe. It is the beauty in the rocks. He does not now refer so much to Himself. He no longer, I think, calls Himself a Him and no longer looks like a man. We no longer share an image of each other. He does not punish us now for not knowing what He wants. He still speaks these things, if you will remember what you have heard, but they are words that have moved through time with us. We hear them now, with or without religion. The words in the rocks are spoken as they are heard. God, who is no idea of God, speaks them now, to us, as we are now. As we encompass the earth, as our religion learns to love others as itself. God speaks to us now if we will listen.

The words in the rocks are before language, and below language. They speak to the stars and dinosaurs and the inland seas of the Cretaceous. They are not spoken to us. They are not for us, though we may listen.

Inside the rocks are words yet unspoken in Air.

13. Sango

AJAKA, KING OF OYO, WAS DEFEATED IN BATTLE BY OLOWU, king of Owu, and a ransom was demanded for his return. Olowu berated Ajaka for ruling improperly and failing to defend Yoruba-land from the Fulanis to the north, while Ajaka accused Olowu of taking advantage of his peaceable nature.

The people of Oyo gathered in the marketplace to grieve the loss of their fallen soldiers while the chiefs met in council to decide how to proceed. Oyo had never paid tribute before to Owu, and no one knew what to do. The Babalawo cast beads on the ground in front of him and said that a messenger should be sent to Ajaka's brother, Sango, who lived in the city of Tapa with his mother's people. He would know what to do.

Tapa is in the land of Nupe. Sango lived there with his two wives, Oba and Osun, and with his mother, Etoorosi, daughter of the king. He was the great-grandson of Oduduwa, founder of the Yoruba kingdom, and a favorite of the gods. They had presented him with a small stone charm that gave him the power of fire and thunder when he put it in his mouth. But Sango was still a young man and unsure of himself. He wanted to learn how to use his powers well. The messenger found him outside the house hurling fireballs from his mouth at an altar a short distance away. The messenger told him he must go quickly to Owu and save his brother Ajaka.

Sango listened to the messenger and consulted the Babalawo on how to proceed. The Ifa oracle advised him to make a sacrifice with a basket of grains and to take some of the grains with him to Owu. Oyo should never submit to Owu, but it would be wrong to continue the war and risk further defeat and bloodshed. As night fell, his wives gathered firewood and stacked it in the center of the courtyard. Drummers appeared, and Sango began dancing around the pile. After circling it three times, he stood back, his cheeks swelled, and flames shot across the courtyard to the base of the pile. As the fire raged, he placed one foot at a time into the fire and, tilting his head back, blew great plumes of flame from his mouth into the night sky. As smoke gathered and swirled about the courtyard, he disappeared into the night without a trace. He reappeared many miles away at the entrance of Olowu's palace in Owu. The king was meeting in council with his chiefs.

Sango came into the palace and knelt on the floor in front of Olowu. "May you live a long life, and may your dictates be just," he said to the Owu king. "May your subjects never desist from following you, and may your enemies know no peace."

"You must bring to my palace fifty baskets of yams, two calabash cans of red palm oil, two horses, and a he-goat to receive your brother," Olowu told him.

"That is impossible!" shouted Sango.

"Impossible? Do it or he will die!"

Sango went outside the palace and raised his hands to the sky in prayer. A storm gathered as his words flew into the night. He reached into his pouch and threw the magic grains on the ground. From where they struck the earth, there arose fifty baskets of yams, two calabash cans of red palm oil, two horses, and a he-goat. Olowu came out from the palace and was amazed. He accepted the ransom and released Ajaka. His mission accomplished, Sango hurried back to Tapa.

But while Ajaka was in exile, his chiefs met again with the Babalawo and asked for a divination as to the status of their king. The Babalawo threw a chain of beads on the floor in front of him and read the message to the chiefs: They would need a new king.

But who? The Babalawo threw the beads again: Someone who does not live in Oyo, the beads read. Who might that be? The Babalawo threw the beads again: The new king would be Sango. "Throw them again," the chiefs demanded. "We require a confirmation." The beads were thrown again: Sango was to be the new king. A messenger was again sent to Nupeland.

As Sango walked through the marketplace on his way back to his mother's house, he saw a young woman with a basket on her head. The sight of her pleased him greatly. He asked people he knew about her, but nobody had seen her before. He introduced himself and said he would like to become acquainted with her and tried to impress her with his royal blood and magical powers. But she turned away and left him standing alone. As she walked across the marketplace and through the town, he followed her with his eyes. As she passed through the city gates and into the forest, he ran to catch up with her, taking care not to be seen. She climbed over a rocky hill a short distance outside the village and stopped at a waterfall. Looking about her in every direction, she removed her clothing and stepped into the stream. With her eyes to the sky, she said something beneath her breath, and a shower of fresh rainwater poured over her. When she was through bathing, the shower ended as suddenly as it began. She stepped out of the stream and walked over to a large overhanging rock at the bottom of the cliff. Removing an antelope skin from under the rock, she put it over her shoulders. As Sango watched from behind a tree, she transformed herself into the antelope and bounded across the stream and into the forest.

Knowing her secret, Sango went to the stream the next day and waited for her. He found the antelope skin beneath the rock and hid it in his bag. After she arrived from the market with the basket on her head, she began to bathe, as before. But when she went to the rock and saw that her skin was missing, she screamed and looked to the sky. "May whoever has taken my skin die a horrible death!" she cried.

Sango stepped out from behind the tree. "Retract the curse!" he demanded. "Retract it now!"

"I retract the curse, but you must promise to give me back my skin!"

"I do not promise."

"Then promise to save my secret. Without it I am nothing. You must promise to save my secret!"

"I promise. But you must promise to live as a human and be my bride."

"I promise."

"You must promise to be faithful and loyal to me always."

"I promise."

"What is your human name?"

"They call me Oya."

"Put on your clothes and come back to the village with me!"

Sango and Oya returned to his mother's house in the village. Oba and Osun were busy pounding yam in the courtyard as he introduced her and instructed them to respect her and to accept her into the household. They were not pleased and continued their work in silence.

Just then the messenger arrived with news that Sango had been chosen the new king of Oyo. The wives were pleased and began dancing and rejoicing with the townspeople. Soon they would be living in the palace in Oyo. There would be a grand coronation, and their husband would be the greatest king in Yorubaland. Sango accepted the news with great dignity, but he remained silent and did not rejoice with the others.

On the day of his coronation Sango told the people of Oyo that he would bring them peace and prosperity. He would seek the favor of the gods and not use warfare to gain wealth and captives. "There are some," he told them, "who attack our villages and frightened our people, and they will be dealt with harshly, but there will be no wars for slaves and riches." Neighboring peoples would not be attacked out of greed. "Only the gods can bring us life," he assured the people. "And I will do all in my power to please them." The people of Oyo were tired of the recent wars and rejoiced at the prospect of many long years of peace under the powerful leadership of their new king.

But Olowu was angry that he was not invited to the coronation and that Sango had accepted the throne of Oyo without his permission. "He should submit to me! He should submit as his brother has submitted," shouted Olowu. "He should pay me tribute! I demand tribute from Oyo! If Sango does not pay me tribute, I will extend my territory up to his palace and make his wives my wives and his children my children. He will know no peace until he submits to me." He instructed his generals to gather the army and began preparing a new attack on Oyo.

In his bedchambers after the coronation, Sango was admiring Oya's hairstyle. He loved the way she pleated it into rows and, loving her as he did, resolved to have his own hair pleated in the same manner. But the Yoruba people believed it was a great abomination for anyone to touch the head of a king.

"Shall I pleat it for you, Sango?" asked Oya.

"Yes, please. Do it now."

As she was working with his hair, Osun entered the room and gasped at what she saw. Sango yelled at her for interrupting and sent her away. Osun ran back to Oba to tell her what she saw, but Oba could not believe it.

"I have never lied to you, Oba," Osun said.

But Oba had to see for herself. As she entered the bedchamber she, too, gasped at the sight of Oya touching the king's head and was sent away. Sango emerged from the bedchamber with his new hairstyle and presented himself to the chiefs. They were amazed that a man would have his hair made as a woman, but they accepted what he had done and admired his audacity.

As they sat in council, the two Oyo generals, Eliri and Oluode, were explaining to Sango that he must prepare to defend Oyo. But Sango was new to the throne and unsure of their loyalty to him. He wanted to fulfill his promise of peace and knew that the generals loved war for the riches it brought them.

As they were speaking, a messenger arrived from Owu demanding tribute. Sango swore he would never submit to Olowu, but before he was able to propose a peaceful solution, Eliri grabbed a knife and killed the messenger. Sango was unable to punish Eliri for this brazen act and grew increasingly suspicious of him. He told the generals to raise an army and prepare a defense, but that he would talk to the Babalawo before making the next move.

The Babalawo told him that he must travel to Ile-Ife and consult the oracle of his father, Orunmiyan, at the great shaft where Oduduwa, his great-grandfather, had descended from the heavens.

As he arrived at the great shaft in Ile-Ife, Orunmiyan appeared to him. "The means to the defense of your kingdom lies in the land of your mother's people. Go to the land of your birth and seek the power from the gods to defend Oyo from Owu. Listen carefully to what you are told."

Sango left Ile-Ife for Nupeland early the next morning. The people of Tapa were overjoyed to see him and prepared a great celebration of dancing and singing. The Babalawo presented him with the gift of a great double-edged battle-ax and informed him that the gods would further strengthen his command of thunder and lightning.

"But there is a woman in your household," he warned, "who commands the rain at will. You must work hand in hand with her. You must listen to her, and you must not misuse the powers that have been granted you." Sango raised the battle-ax to the sky in thanks to the gods as bolts of lightning lit the clouds and thunder rolled across the earth. He now had the means to provide security to his people and wise counsel about how to use it. He returned at once to Oyo.

While he was gone, Osun and Oba scolded Oya repeatedly for touching the head of the king. They accused her of violating tradition, and she answered with insults. The argument raged as Sango arrived at the palace gate. He became angry with all of them and accused them of distracting him from more important business. Osun and Oba insisted that he send Oya away, but Sango refused. Fire began flying from his mouth as his anger grew, and flames shot across the room. Oya was alarmed and quickly stepped in to quiet him, soothing him with songs and gentle words. As his rage ebbed and he regained control of his powers, news arrived that Owu soldiers were at the city gates. Sango turned to Oya. She reached her arms to the sky and a great rainstorm fell to the earth. Sango answered with bolts of thunder and lightning. The storm's violence drove the enemy soldiers away, and the city was saved.

But this was only the beginning of the war. The warriors of Oyo, lead by Eliri and Oluode, filed out through the city gates and into the forest to find the enemy. Sango and his wives accompanied them. They crossed the river and stopped in a clearing for a midday meal of roasted yams.

But the army of Owu lay in ambush. The women were busy serving the soldiers as the attack came, and there was no time to prepare a defense. Sango called on the power of the lightning and blew great bolts of fire toward the advancing army, sending them reeling back into the forest. As his army braced for a second assault, Sango gathered a handful of grain from Oya's pouch belt. Placing the grains on his double-edged battle-ax, he blew them off into the sky, where they became vampire bats. The bats circled overhead and attacked the oncoming Owu, defeating them soundly as the battle raged.

The enemy lay in defeat and the warriors of Oyo sang and danced at the great victory they had won. Sango raised the battle-ax a second time, and the bats circled and returned, landing on the ax one by one, turning back into grains. But as the last of the bats landed, it warned Sango that there was an uprising at home in Oyo. Sango poured the magic grains back into Oya's pouch and announced to the army that they would have to return to Oyo immediately.

But Eliri and Oluode insisted that the army follow through on its great victory by attacking Owu itself. "The king of Owu must be captured. His palace must be swept clean of his possessions. We must reverse our recent losses and avenge the humiliation of Ajaka!" they shouted. "We need the wealth of Owu in our own houses! We need captives! We need more slaves!"

Sango shouted back angrily, "You must obey me and return to Oyo."

But the soldiers were roused in the drunkenness of their victory. Soon they were shouting with Eliri and Oluode. "On to Owu! Avenge our king Ajaka!"

Sango looked to the sky and raised his two-edge battle-ax in anger. His mouth swelled ready to throw fire, but Oya placed her hand over it.

"No. You must not use your powers in this manner. You must not use it against your own people. Come, let us see about this uprising in Oyo."

Most of the army followed Eliri and Oluode to Owu, while Sango, his wives, and a small band of followers returned to Oyo. As they reached the palace gates, they saw a large crowd chanting in protest against the ongoing war with Owu. *"Awa o f'ogun mo!"* they chanted. *"Awa o f'ogun mo! No more war! No more war!"*

"Too many of us are widows," the women were saying. "These children are all orphans. Too many of our sons have died! Let us make peace with Olowu. Let us return to our normal lives with those we love! Let us have an end to these wars!"

Sango entered the palace and retired to his bedchamber. Oya entered the room.

"Half of my people want war. The other half does not. Neither will follow me. What should I do?"

"They love you, Sango. They will follow you if you are wise. Do not worry about the foolish things they do."

But Sango rose and began pacing the floor, first one way and then the other. "They should follow what I say. I am their king! They should obey me!" His face was puffed in anger.

"Do not worry about them. They will follow you. You must be wise and do what is best for them." He stopped and stared in her face. "Sango," she said. "You must give me the stone charm, that I may keep it in a safe place."

"No! I must have the power of fire with me to deal with my enemies!"

"So long as it is in your possession, you will have the urge to use it in anger. Listen to the voice of your people."

"The charm is the source of my power."

"I will keep it for you and give it back when you need it."

"But what if you lose it? What if you cannot find it when I need it? What if you are not loyal to me?"

"I will keep it here, in my pouch belt. I have promised to be loyal to you. I am your wife and you are my master."

Sango stood up, looking to the sky. His cheeks suddenly swelled as if he were ill, and he spat the stone into his hand. He looked at it for a long time, and then handed it to Oya. "You have spoken wisely. You must keep this in a safe place."

Eliri and Oluode soon returned from Owu, laden with the captured wealth of their enemies. "We have only taken back what you gave them in ransom," they told Sango. But Sango was more suspicious than ever. He decided to send them away to distant villages as "gatekeepers," where they would watch the frontiers. Eliri refused to go, stating that he deserved more than a gate-keeper's post for his gallantry and for all that he had done for Oyo. But Oluode agreed to go because, as he told his friend Eliri, "I disobeyed Sango one time on the field of battle. I will not disobey him a second time."

Oluode traveled with a small band of soldiers to the city of Ede. The people there feared him and made him king, even though there were others still living who were in line for the throne. When Sango heard what happened, he thought of a way to eliminate both generals. He sent Eliri with orders to kill Oluode for illegally assuming the position of king. When Eliri arrived in Ede and told Oluode his orders, Oluode laughed and said, "Surely you will not kill your friend?"

"I have already disobeyed Sango one time on the field of battle," Eliri replied. "I will not disobey him a second time." But instead of killing him, he took Oluode captive and brought him back to Oyo.

Sango was disappointed. "You have captured Oluode, but you have not followed my orders!"

"I could not violate the bounds of friendship."

"Very well. Then you will fight him to the death, in public."

The two were dragged to the center of town and forced to fight. Eliri cast a spell on Oluode and killed him with his knife.

Turning to Sango he said, "It is clear you wanted my death. But I demand now that you abdicate the throne! You must abdicate the throne of our forefathers! If you are still evident in Oyo as the next moon fills, I will personally despoil your tomb!"

Sango retreated to the palace. In the bedchamber he asked Oya for the charm. "I must have it now. Eliri is preparing to overthrow me. Give me the charm."

"I must have some time to find it."

"I will have it now!"

"But you do not need fire to deal with Eliri."

"Give it to me now!"

"I do not know where it is."

"It is here, in your pouch belt." Sango reached into the pouch and grabbed the stone charm. "It is wet! You have kept it with your other charms of the stream and of the rain, and it has gotten wet! It will lose its potency! Why have you kept it this way, foolish woman? I must see what power it may still have."

"No! Sango! Do not test it! You should not use it in that manner!"

Sango ran out of the palace and climbed the high hill just outside the city gate. When he got to the top, he swallowed the charm and raised his hands to the sky. "Let us see what potency remains!" he shouted, as the storm gathered. "The charm has gotten wet. Let us see what remains of my powers!"

As he spoke, a bolt of lightning crashed from the sky and hit the city below. The palace exploded in flames. He watched as people ran screaming out of their houses and through the city gates.

"What have I done?" he shouted, looking down on the city. "Is this what my powers have done for me?" He ran back down the hill to where many of his people lay dead and dying, including his own children. "I will not reenter the city gates," he said aloud but to himself. "I do not deserve this kingdom. I do not deserve this life ever again." He turned and started toward the forest.

But Oba, Osun, and Oya had run through the gates and escaped the fire. They saw him as he turned and ran after him. "Sango! Stop! Come back! We need you!" they cried.

"No! Go back!" he commanded.

"Please! Come back to us. Do not leave!"

"Go back! Go away!" he shouted and walked into the forest.

"All is lost," said Oya to Oba and Osun.

"No," they assured her. "We will recover."

"But the children are all lost."

"What? The children?"

"Yes, all the children are lost."

Oba and Osun screamed in despair. Turning away from each other, they ran separate ways into the forest. Oya turned and ran after Sango but never found him in this world. He was never seen again.

Some say Sango hanged himself from a tree in repentance. Others say that he walked all the way to Koso, and they deny that he ever died. But those who know him say that he still speaks from the sky whenever the clouds gather.

"I did not hang. I live on and provide guidance and security to my people. I forgive my adversaries who walk in honor."

But those who understand the thunder know that there is no meaning to his shouts and bursts of anger without the rains of Oya and the life-giving streams of Oba and Osun.

14. Valley of the Gods

TWO DAYS AGO, AT CHESLER PARK, I LISTENED TO THE ROCKS
one at a time. From east to north and back, higher or lower, then
south to west, up and back, farther and nearer, I carefully scanned
each shape and color. I saw each and passed on to the next, in
whatever direction, without plan or order. But there was a broken,
linear quality to the strata. Corresponding to time, it gave a nat-
ural order to the movement of the eye. The words were in any
direction, through gaps and leaps in the space that still is, but
there was a unitary quality to the message.

But here, at Valley of the Gods, there are many songs. The
Earth here, rising through Permian seawater, sings now the words
of many songs, each butte and spire a separate god.

I was taught in my youth not to believe this, not to think it. I
was taught the unity of the Godhead and believed it and believe
it still. But here I see also that God is many. I do not believe or
not believe it. There is no point either way. I listen to what the
rocks say and there is no question as to belief.

Man is small here. Man cannot be seen here. I am looking at a
hundred million years of rock: Where is man? I am not reading
about it or thinking about it, I am looking at it. It is right here
before me. Over there is eight million years, and here, fifteen mil-
lion. Above is another thirty million, and below where I sit is a
thousand million years of the Grand Canyon. Where is man?
Where is our stratum? I am told that these formations erode at
about a quarter inch every hundred years — seven inches since

the time of Abraham, Isaac, and Jacob. Seven inches! I am looking out over thirty miles of desert — where is seven inches? I cannot see seven inches from here.

I do not believe God created man in time. I believe that God and man created the concept of each other and that these hills were here before then. I believe that God created the hills before He created Himself and man. I know it.

When Abraham crossed the desert from the land of Shinar, he stopped and knelt in the dust and saw God. God and Abraham became one thing, and God filled the vessel of Abraham.

That is how we know of God. We know what Abraham told us. He is our side of the story, one of us, one who speaks the words of language, telling of meaning and truth that we cannot always see. And Abraham founded a great nation, and his seed filled the land — two lands — and lives on through his peoples and through the jealousy of their God. There are no other gods before Him.

Since the time of Abraham, these canyons and hills have washed back seven or eight inches. They do not say now exactly what they said then. They are still here, their caps and high spires of coarse sandstone over sloping skirts of gravel and shale, somewhat smaller now, with fins and ledges gone. The songs are much the same. Were Abraham here, he would hear them and tell us the meaning.

He was, in fact, here. He was not Abraham, but he was here, listening to the rocks. We do not know what God told him — or her — but we may listen now.

I believe in God as I believe in the reality of the rocks I am looking at now. I believe that they exist in the mind of God and that they are His thoughts and words. That is what God is and what He does. But I do not believe He made them. I do not believe they were made 250 million years ago, or on the third day, or whatever. I believe He makes them now as I see them. He creates and is the experience of seeing them as they are. They are not here these millions of years waiting for me, or Abraham, or some Anasazi ancestor to look their way. They are now, as I listen and as you hear. There was no now then, and there is no language now of then.

There was language then of then, and there were people, and the buttes and canyons then were much as they are now. There was a then then because I have been told of it and believe it. There were fish and amphibians here when these rocks were laid down, and dinosaurs and mammals later on, but I only know what I have been told. I remember being told these things, and that they are as real as what I see.

I listen now to God speak the Universe as morning light creeps into folds and crevices of ancient sandstone, and I know that this is not all He is saying. I say what I hear, and I create, or reveal, an idea of God that is, I think, true and pure, but it is an idea of God. God gave Abraham an idea and more, teaching him how to keep his people together through thousands of years. And He revealed Himself to the Anasazi and the Navaho. It is how He sings to me now in voices of polytheistic harmony. God needs us to speak language. I do not believe He knows how without us. We are the language of God — the words that have seeped out of the rocks and into the mind of man.

But we have too many words. We have heard our own words for so long that we think them more real than the rocks from which they became Air. We think the rocks become real when we give them names. We create God from our words. It is time to listen again.

The flocks are gathered, the Philistines defeated, and the temptations of Baal now past. It is time to listen again. Thank you, O Lord, for bringing us this far. Thank you now for the echo of your words from the desert. I am small and cannot know what You are saying all around me. I am hungry and fed; I thirst, and there is water. There are thoughts running through my mind, thoughts of other places and times that I cannot control, distracting my *perfect attention from Your words, but I hear them. I see thought rising and boiling in my mind as I see the line of Cedar Mesa in the distant west. I see the ripples in my mind and in the valleys and canyons and dry washes of the desert. I see the weight of the mesas on the desert floor, and I feel the ache in my bones. My thoughts arise and vanish; yours remain. But I listen. I listen and will try to say, though it is only words and not rocks. There is a love from you, dear God, that transcends these indifferent rocks.*

And there is a world before us. The word of God lives through the language of the Bible, but it is time to read the rocks again. What are we, dear God, that has circled the earth and made cities of forest and plain? What are we, that dig into Earth for light and motion? Who are we that see the surfaces of planets and galaxies at the edge of time? How is it that we may uncreate language, uncreate ourselves that you have given us? How is it that we must now care? How may we let birds fly through the forest? We are no longer the shepherds of Canaan, dear God. We are at the edge of extinction, the very edge, and there is nothing but your aware- ness of us that will live on with these rocks around me. We cannot go on as we are. A straight line from who we have been through who we are now leads to extinction, dear God; we can see that. We can see that from here. What is it you would have us become?

The rocks will go on either way. The human stratum will be thin, barely visible, unnoticed in all these layers and layers of sandstone and shale. The human stratum will be thin — dark, perhaps — but the rock will go on through time. Language will be no more, but the rock will go on. I accept that. I accept that for myself — for should the human stratum grow thicker, I will not know it. I accept my fate and that of my kind.

But there is a surge of energy that is not rock or language that uplifts the layers of weight in my mind — that is not of my mind but of the mind of humanity. It is the will to live and to live well on the earth. It is the energy of self-preservation and of love for living things that comes at once and in one form. It is not from outside. It is not God the Father. It is not a chastening, jealous god, who will part the seas for us and close them for others. But neither is it my idea nor yours, and I can say no more. It will not save us. God will not save us. Nor will we save ourselves without Him. We will or will not become aware of how big we now are and how small, and of the womb still around us, and of living things emerging with us. We will see through the words of the Bible and of the rocks, watching the metamorphosis of rock into new language.

Dear God, we kneel before you in the sand.

You will not know the energy in me by reading a book or by looking at the rocks. They just sit there. You will not know what I mean by God if there is a stronger idea in you. And I will not know how deeply you believe it. I am but a ripple in one of these hills — and not even that.

Part IV — The Beautiful

15. America the Powerful

Oh powerful, for thunderous skies!
For amber waves of men.
America! America!

AMERICA THE POWERFUL! IT IS TO FLATTER YOU THAT I WRITE: you, who see yourself in a cold, imperialist mirror of altruism; you, who resist most what is best for Americans and for all people.

America the Powerful is bullets and tanks and hydrogen bombs. It is our national ego — the *us* that defines itself against *them* — the team that needs another team to play against. It is the part of America that thinks it is bigger and better and badder than anyone else: the part that needs an enemy to be what it is. America the Powerful has no meaning without an enemy. And when there is no enemy, it will create one.

America the Powerful used to be the same thing as America the Beautiful. From the first musket shot on Lexington Green until the last three days of World War II, we had to be powerful to be beautiful. We had to defend freedom. We had to be independent. We drew a line where America ended and non-America began. We were prepared to kill non-Americans to be American ourselves.

America the Powerful saved us and kept us safe, but it cannot save us now. It no longer preserves life, liberty, and the pursuit of happiness as it did in the days of Jefferson, Madison, and Roosevelt.

Security is still the number one function of government, but it is global security that will save us and not national security.

In the twenty-first century, all nations will lose the dream of global hegemony; America will lose the reality. For America the Powerful, this will be the worst possible course of events; for America the Beautiful, it will be a blessing. The vision of invincibility, the power of pride, the assurance of being number one — these will all pass. The spacious skies and purple mountains will live on. God will no longer bless America at the expense of her enemies, but He will shed His grace on the fruited plain, and brotherhood will shine from sea to sea and beyond.

It is the passive use of power that Americans will miss and not its active burden. Americans will be relieved to be rid of their role as world policemen. But power, or the potential for violence, whether openly exercised or held in reserve, underlies all political relations and all forms of human organization. It is what makes us who we are in the collective sense. When America no longer has it, Americans will not be what they now are. The loss of power will occur at a profound level of consciousness and only with a fight — a fight that Americans will lose. But they will see their ideas, their history, and their culture incorporated into the new world order more than those of any other nation. America the Beautiful will live on.

America is bigger than America. It is bigger that ourselves as a separate people. If we claim it as a possession and defend it against non-Americans, it will shrivel and die. If we cross-pollinate it with the traditions of other peoples, we will create a world society capable of addressing real world problems. If we waste our treasure and the lives of our young people on bombs and bullets and aircraft carriers trying to keep ourselves apart from others, we will die by the sword that is in our hands.

How will America the Beautiful live on? When our national ego is no longer attached, our ideals will be human ideals that took root first in America. When we are people who happen to be American, our genius for federalism, for democracy, and for conscious creation of new government will be universal. Our gift of popular government and popular culture will be received by all others and belong to them. America the Beautiful is not ours to keep; it becomes our beauty only as we give it to the world and thereby return it to ourselves.

America the Powerful is our separation from, and violence toward, human beings who are not American. It has no place in the future. It is America the Beautiful that will evolve with the rest of human civilization.

16. Lexington Green

Parker led those of us who were equipped to the north end of
Lexington Common, near the Bedford Road, and formed us in
single file. I was stationed about in the centre of the company.
While we were standing, I left my place and went from one
end of the company to the other and counted every man who
was paraded, and the whole number was thirty-eight, and no
more.[10]

— *Sylvanus Wood, minuteman*

We arrived there and saw a number of people, I believe
between 200 and 300, formed in a common in the middle of
the town. We still continued advancing, keeping prepared
against an attack tho' without intending to attack them; but
on our coming near them they fired one or two shots, upon
which our men without any orders rushed in upon them, fired
and put 'em to flight.[11]

— *Lieutenant John Barker, British Officer*

BARKER CLAIMED TO HAVE SEEN 200 TO 300 AMERICANS AT
Lexington Green; Wood, 38.

The officer came up to within about two rods of the centre of
the company, where I stood...[he] swung his sword, and said,
"Lay down your arms, you damned rebels, or you are all dead
men. Fire! ... There was not a gun fired by any of Captain
Parker's company, within my knowledge. I was so situated
that I must have known it....[12]

— *Sylvanus Wood*

Wood and Parker were the first Americans. They and those who stood with them on the green in the face of deliberate death were the first to die to themselves as British colonists and risk rebirth as American patriots. They were the first who were who we are.

It was the British who made them American: men in red coats, standing together, with powder charges behind iron balls, sighting along hollow iron tubes at the vital organs of men. It was they who created America. They killed us and made us more than what we were. Without them there would have been nothing against which to be what we have become.

War tells us who we are. We are the people who stood with Parker in Lexington, with Travis at the Alamo, who stormed the beaches at Iwo Jima and Normandy. We are the ones who won, or who lost desperately — the ones who rose above our separate selves to become a great nation. We need not have been there.

War sorts people out: the hero from the enemy, the brave from the timid. Without war, we would not be sure where we stand or if we would stand. War wrenches us from the tedium of everyday life, challenges us to be all that we can be. It complicates circumstance and simplifies commitment. Legal murder, heroic murder, compulsory murder: It gives us purpose, something to die for and something to live for. War elevates the intensity of life to a point where it is worth living. Love, family, country, religion, devotion, principle — all of these are elevated in time of war. The greatest literary creations of all nations are inspired by the risking of self to a higher cause: novels, poems, movies, plays, love stories of war, war stories of love. War is the greatest altruism, the greatest possible sacrifice, the purest gift to others. The red badge can have no ulterior motive.

The identity of self in nationhood gained through experience in battle is the most fundamental identity of our time. It is more profound than class, race, religion, or ideology. But it is an identity that exists only in opposition to some other human identity:

There must be a redcoat to make a patriot, a Serb to make a Croat, a Greek and a Russian to make a Turk. There has to be someone who is not what you are. The self discovered in battle is always a negative of the enemy, and the enemy is always human. We are all Turks or Americans or Russians because somebody else is not and cannot be.

We have no control over this. We have no control over the size of the earth and its continents and oceans and ranges of mountains. We did not determine its axis or ordain its diameter and gravity. It is not we who made the earth large enough for separate societies and small enough for humans to orbit it in an hour. We did not make it strong enough to absorb musket fire and weak enough to melt in the core of atoms. We did not set the scale of terrestrial geography. We would on our own, perhaps, have made it a little larger. Large enough to contain us, as we now are, with the tools and weapons we have made. Large enough to let us be less than fully human. But we have no control over this. The Earth was made once and for all, and there is no more of it. It has closed in on our separateness. There is nowhere else to go to be what we have been.

Nuclear energy and intercontinental weaponry will create a cataclysmic upheaval in human identity. When they strike, we will not know who we are. There will be no one we are not. The loss of warfare will mean a loss of the greatest experience in human life and the most profound understanding of what life is about. There will be no transcendence of self against other people. Those who live through the annihilation will die to what they now are.

17. The Declaration of Interdependence

When, in the course of human events, it becomes necessary for one people to dissolve the political bands which have connected them with another, and to assume among the powers of the earth the separate and equal station to which the laws of nature and of nature's God entitle them, a decent respect to the opinions of mankind requires that they should declare the causes which impel them to the separation.

We hold these truths to be self-evident: that all men are created equal; that they are endowed by their Creator with certain unalienable rights; that among these are life, liberty, and the pursuit of happiness; that, to secure these rights, governments are instituted among men, deriving their just powers from the consent of the governed; that whenever any form of government becomes destructive of these ends, it is the right of the people to alter or abolish it...

FOR JEFFERSON, AND FOR OTHERS OF HIS TIME, GOD CREated man in a "state of nature" — that is, without any government at all. Everyone had absolute freedom; no one had the right to tell anyone else what to do or what not to do. Each person could do what he or she had the personal power to accomplish, or in other words, whatever he could get away with. If a person wanted to take another's life, liberty, or property, there was nothing to stop him. If you are bigger than I am, you can come through my door and help yourself to whatever you want, including me.

There is no piece of paper in a courthouse saying you cannot do that and no police force or body of outraged citizenry to protect me. If I can escape you, I might as well go over to your house and steal your things while you are stealing mine. In fact, in a state of nature, there can be no difference between what is yours and what is mine.

But God also "endowed" each person with the right to his or her own life, freedom, and property. (Jefferson meant "property" by "pursuit of happiness," but the word sounded too crass. John Locke, his predecessor, used the more blunt "life, liberty, and property" to justify the English Revolution of some four score and seven years earlier.) But God did not create any way of "securing" these rights; that was the business of man himself. Man instituted government to protect what God gave him.

Government, then, is a "social contract" in which we each give up some measure of freedom — particularly that of violating others — in order to secure protection for ourselves. You give up your freedom to kill, enslave, or steal from me (even if you are bigger), and I give up the same freedoms with respect to you. The rest of human history is concerned with how we define what belongs to each of us and who gets to protect whom. But because we "choose" to make government, we may choose also to unmake it. We may decide whether or not it is working for us. This does not mean that we are merely allowed to criticize the policy of a particular government or to vote somebody out of office — it means that we can do away with the government *entirely* when it does not protect who we are and what we have. It gives us the fundamental right to revolution. This is what the Declaration of Independence is all about.

The Declaration is more fundamental than the American Constitution. According to Jefferson, if Americans wish to overthrow the Constitution, they may do so. (Even though "…governments long established should not be changed for light and transient causes.…") To the extent that the Declaration applies outside of

America — and the opening sentence makes clear that it does — it also gives all people, everywhere, the right to overthrow any government that does not protect them. People may choose at any time to go back to the state of nature or to pass back through it to something else whenever the government they have created does not do what it was created to do.

Jefferson leaves the impression in the Declaration that the creation or destruction of a government is a conscious, deliberate, and logical process. We know, however, that it is also always confusing and violent. Existing governments never step down without a fight, and it is never entirely clear during a revolution who is fighting whom and for what. The Declaration led to a bewildering confusion of loyalties among British Americans — just as many sided with the king as actively fought against him — and it led to six more years of gruesome warfare. But there is no real contradiction here. What Jefferson and his friends were doing in Philadelphia in July of 1776 was, in fact, conscious, deliberate, and logical — it was the state of nature they brought about that was confusing and violent. In deliberately repudiating the social contract with the king of England, they led Americans into the horror of absolute freedom.

Chaotic as it is, there can be no known path through the state of nature to some other social contract. Once it is entered, anything can happen. Personalities, chance occurrences, or minor skirmishes can throw the entire weight of a nation's history in one direction or another. Logic has no place; the only consideration is of power. All of the thought and deliberation in the world that precipitates a revolutionary process will have no bearing on its outcome except insofar as it maintains a focus of power. Reason can never win a revolution; it can only inspire the irrational acts by which a revolution is won.

This is what the Declaration of Independence did for the American Revolution. By July fourth of 1776, the war was already more than a year old. The battles of Lexington, Concord, and

Bunker Hill had already been fought, and the movement was well under way in Maine, Canada, North Carolina, and Charleston Bay. Hundreds were already dying for the cause, and many thousands more were willing to die, but there was general confusion as to what it was all about. Those who took part knew what they were fighting against but not what they were fighting for. Into the early months of 1776, most claimed to be defending their rights *as Englishmen*. There are reports that in January of that year, Washington's officers were still toasting the king's health. There was anger, hatred, and a longing for liberty from existing political forms, but there was no sense of where the future might lie.

Jefferson sensed that the future was as yet unimportant, and his Declaration made no attempt to address it. Instead he addressed the present: that we are fighting not against a policy, but against government itself; that we are fighting for the right to fight against, for the right to not have government. At some point, Americans will "...institute new government, laying its foundation on such principles, and organizing its powers in such form, as to them shall seem most likely to affect their safety and happiness..." — but not now. Now we must uncivilize ourselves. Now we must discard all attributes of society and religion, brutalize our enemies and ourselves, kill and be killed, and plunge headlong into the forest of fear and darkness. There can be no clear vision of the future. Only if we are sufficiently savage and inhuman need we worry about instituting new government.

––

People do not desire the state of nature. But they are willing to risk it, consciously and deliberately, when government fails to protect them. The taxes and abuses of the British colonial government seem mild when compared to the dangers that now face the prospect of continued human habitation of the earth. Government need not be bad to be inadequate.

July 4, 2003

America's message to the world is universal. What it says about itself applies to other peoples and to other moments in history. As global civilization evolves in the twenty-first century, the American message will become less particularly American.

This will be a great problem for the people of America. What we have always understood to be our own will be taken from us and distributed generally. We will feel both flattered and exploited. How well we adapt to a changing status will depend on our maturity as a nation.

> When, in the course of human events, it becomes necessary for all peoples of the world to band together to prevent war among nations and to act in wholeness toward the earth, and to assume, among the species of the earth, the rightful station to which the laws of nature and of nature's God entitle them, a decent respect to the opinions of humankind requires that they should declare the causes which impel them to the unity.

Now is a pivotal time. A crisis has arisen to which we must respond or perish. We have to redefine who we are and how we relate to ourselves and to those who we are not. There is a natural order in the universe to which we must adjust. We should tell the world what we are thinking.

> We hold these truths to be self-evident: that all people are created equal; that they are endowed by their Creator with certain unalienable rights, that among these are life, liberty and the pursuit of happiness; that to secure these rights, governments are instituted among people, deriving their just powers from the consent of the governed; that whenever any form of government becomes destructive of these ends, it is the right of the people to alter or to abolish it, and to institute new government, laying its foundation on such principles and organizing its powers in such form, as to them shall seem most likely to effect their safety and happiness.

God did not create government — we did, for the purpose of preserving what God *did* create: freedom, equality, and life itself. When government does not serve its intended purpose — by failing to keep us free, equal, or alive; or by enslaving us or endangering our lives — we may uncreate what we have created and start over. We have the right to revolution. This is not an opinion; it is a fundamental truth obvious to any who care to look.

The history of independent national sovereignty is a history of repeated wars, environmental destruction, and transgressions of individual liberties. To prove this, let facts be submitted to a candid world.

It has caused the deliberate and unconscionable perpetration of hatred among the diverse peoples of the earth.

It has caused the deliberate and unconscionable death of hundreds of millions of men and women in military service.

It has caused the incidental and unconscionable death of hundreds of millions of civilian men, women, and children in times of war.

It has caused injury, starvation, poverty, and homelessness to billions of men, women, and children in times of war.

It has caused the destruction of family life for billions of human beings.

It has caused the depletion of the treasuries of the various nations in the maintenance of large standing armies at the expense of social and humanitarian need.

It has distorted the proper social development of billions of young people by quartering them in isolated camps and training them to kill and be killed in the name of nationality.

It has caused the neglect of the world's environment.

It has divided nation against nation in the global care of forests, oceans, and the atmosphere.

It has caused rampant misuse and depletion of the earth's resources by allowing artificially low world prices in nations without proper environmental legislation.

It has caused loss of vocation among laborers in developed countries and exploitation of labor in underdeveloped countries by allowing artificially low wages in nations without just and appropriate labor laws.

It has allowed the torture and death of innumerable human individuals by denying them the protection of international standards of justice.

It has allowed the growth of international terrorism by depriving the world of a just and uniform system of law enforcement.

It has allowed the proliferation of nuclear weapons by attempting to justify their possession by some nations and not by others, and by failing to control trade of fissile material.

The current form of government is inappropriate. It has failed to protect against violence and to regulate our enterprises in a just and healthy manner. Its scope and reach have not kept pace with modern communications and weaponry. It continues to divide us against ourselves at a time when we are most capable of killing or being killed by each other. We will not long survive with this form of government.

We, therefore, the good peoples of this Earth, appealing to the Supreme Judge of the world for the rectitude of our intentions, declare that it is our right, it is our duty, to throw off such government, and to provide new guards for our future security. We acknowledge the historic significance and past propriety of the independent nation–state, but affirm in the present age the intercontinental dimension of communications, commerce, and weaponry, and assert that no nation may continue to exist, in spirit or in practice, as a separate part of the earth or of the earth's people. We do, therefore, solemnly publish and declare that all human beings are, and of right ought to be, free and interdependent, and that they are absolved from all allegiance to the divisions of humankind. We further declare that, as the united Peoples of the World, we have full power to wage Peace, repress war, illegalize weapons of mass destruction, regulate the manufacture and trade of all other weapons of military use, create just and democratic systems of international justice and law enforcement, establish uniform laws of labor and commerce, tend and care for the lands, seas, and air of the planet, preserve undeveloped spaces for non-human species, regulate resource extraction, protect the planetary environment, and to do all other acts and things which a united and democratic humanity may of right do. And for the support of this Declaration, with a firm reliance on the protection of Divine Providence, we mutually pledge to each other our lives, our fortunes, and our sacred honor.

We have outgrown the form of government that now exists and declare that we are no longer bound by it. We understand the gravity of this step and do not take it lightly. We appeal to God and to the conscience of humanity to acknowledge the purity of our intentions. We claim the right also to create an entirely new form of government that will protect us from war, injustice, and the destruction of commercial and environmental anarchy. We understand and accept the danger this step brings to our own lives and liberties.

Childhood is the age of dependence, adolescence of independence, and adulthood of interdependence.

18. The Connecticut Compromise

Philadelphia, August 1787

We the people of the United States, in order to form a more perfect union, establish justice, insure domestic tranquility, provide for the common defense, promote the general welfare, and secure the blessings of liberty to ourselves and our posterity, do ordain and establish this Constitution for the United States of America.

THIS IS NOT ENTIRELY TRUE. WE THE PEOPLE DID NOT MAKE the federal Constitution of the United States. "We" neither wrote nor ratified it. It was imposed on us by our state governments.

Popular sentiment at the time was deeply divided, and had there been a direct popular vote for or against the constitution, there is not much doubt that it would have failed. Thomas Jefferson was skeptical and out of the country at the time (though he later gave the Constitution his blessing). Patrick Henry "smelled a rat," and George Mason, Richard Henry Lee, and George Clinton were all firmly against it. There were riots against it in Philadelphia and in rural areas of New York, Pennsylvania, and Maryland. We the people were having something done to us that we did not entirely understand or consent to.

To this day it is our states, and not we ourselves, who can add to or subtract from the Constitution. No American citizen, as an individual, has ever in all our history directly voted for any measure by which we constitute ourselves as a nation. To what, then, does the Constitution owe its legitimacy?

Before the constitution, sovereignty was in the hands of state governments. It had been won from the British Empire as the "united colonies" named in the Declaration of Independence became "free and independent states." But the former colonies were independent from each other as well as from the mother country. The "United States" was a plural and not a singular noun, and any new constitutional arrangement would have to take this fundamental truth into account. Sovereignty would flow from the *states* and not from the people. The states had acted together on occasion but not as a single sovereign unit. The central government, such as it was, drew its authority from the Articles of Confederation, drafted and ratified by the states during the war, more as means of coordinating the immediate effort against the British than as a permanent constitutional arrangement. Each state retained the right to levy taxes, declare war, issue currency, regulate commerce, promote justice, and each retained the ultimate loyalty of its citizens. The Continental Congress embodied the nation as a whole but was more an association of state governments than a truly national government. It had no real governing powers and no claim to direct loyalty from individuals. There was no executive or judicial authority and no dependable means of raising funds. The bonds it had issued during the war were "not worth a Continental." Congress had to beg the states for voluntary contributions to meet its financial obligations, usually without result. The central government was, in fact, little more than a league of sovereign states. The United States of the late 1700s resembled in many ways the United Nations of late 1900s.

Individual citizens of New York or Virginia were New Yorkers or Virginians first and Americans second. Forced to choose between state and country, they would have chosen their state. Being "American" meant what being "Slavic" or "African" means today: a geographic proximity, a common culture and history, and an emotional attachment but no common sovereignty. There was no America that could keep citizens from fighting each other when the vital interests of their separate states were at risk, as there is now no world entity that can keep citizens from fighting in the name of their separate nations.

The greatest problem faced at the Constitutional Convention was not democracy or commercial aristocracy or civil liberties but how to keep the states from conflicting with each other. Some means had to be devised whereby people from large and small states would begin to feel the importance of being American over being any particular type of American and begin to transfer allegiance to the country as a whole.

Before the Constitution went into effect, states often fought over boundaries and issues of territorial expansion. Connecticut contested borders with Massachusetts and Rhode Island; Virginia claimed territories also claimed by North Carolina, South Carolina, and Georgia, and it was close to war with Pennsylvania on the eve of the Revolution. South Carolina and Georgia disputed lands to their west (now Mississippi and Alabama) as did Virginia, New York, and Pennsylvania. New York, New Hampshire, and Massachusetts all disputed ownership of what later became Vermont.

The state of New York warned settlers west of the Connecticut River against accepting grants from New Hampshire, but the towns responded by forming committees of safety to defend themselves from New York as much as from the British, claiming to "wholly renounce and resist the administration of the government of New York." Several towns along the east bank of the Connecticut River tried to secede from New Hampshire and join Vermont. There was violence and bloodshed among settlers and militia of Vermont and New York. Ethan Allen, the hero of Vermont independence, attacked and disbanded a settlement of New Yorkers at Otter Creek. He later crossed over the Green Mountains with the Vermont militia to defend against an incursion of "Yorkers" at

Brattleboro and Guilford.[13] He was as determined against New York as he was against Britain during the Revolution:

> Those...who have suffered so much from Yorkish and British tyranny, will yet take the field against the government of New-York (if need be) and at the muzzle of their firelocks convince them of the independency of the state of Vermont.[14]

The most serious armed conflict between states occurred between citizens of Connecticut and Pennsylvania in the Wyoming Valley of north-central Pennsylvania. Connecticut's royal charter of 1662 gave her domain all the way to the Pacific Ocean, excepting lands belonging to New York. But Penn's charter of 1681 gave these same lands to Pennsylvania.

The disputed territory, lying in the upper Susquehanna River Valley, was purchased from the Six Iroquois Nations in 1754 by a Connecticut land company. Two hundred Connecticut families made the trip westward in 1762, but they were forced to leave by unfriendly Indians. In their absence, Pennsylvanians persuaded the Indians to renounce the Connecticut deed and occupied the area with an armed party. A new wave of Connecticut settlers arrived in 1769, and an armed conflict ensued in which the Pennsylvanians were routed. This became known as the First Pennite War of 1771. The Connecticut militia repulsed the Pennsylvanians again a few years later in the Second Pennite War, as described by their commander, Colonel Zebulun Butler:

> They [The Pennites] had six or seven hundred men, two cannon &c. I marched with about four hundred of my regiment, which I thought enough for seven hundred of such wretches. As soon as they came in sight, they fired without saying a word, and rushed to surround us. Our people met them with as much resolution, and a very heavy fire ensued. We soon drove them, killed a number, and drove one wing of the body into the mountains; the main body retreated. This was the 21st of December [1775]....

On the 23rd...as their boat came to shore, with about one hundred men, our people poured in the shot upon them.... They had fifty or sixty killed or wounded. We had two killed and three wounded, one of which is since dead.[15]

By 1776, the Wyoming Valley became Westmoreland County of the State of Connecticut. It paid Connecticut taxes, obeyed Connecticut laws, and lived under the rule of Connecticut courts. Its citizens were committed to a Connecticut identity, and the militia was kept in a constant state of readiness. Congress attempted to deal with the dispute in 1782 by appointing a five-judge panel to settle the question. The court ruled unanimously in favor of Pennsylvania, and the state established a new civil administration for the valley.

But violence continued. A Pennsylvania-based land company with rival claims invaded the area with two companies of soldiers and began evicting Connecticut families from their land by force of arms. A bloody war ensued, with evictions, burnings, and murders. By May 1784, the settlers were pushed all the way to the Delaware River, and the Pennsylvania militia was called out to put an end to the violence.

Out of sympathy for the settlers, the Pennsylvania legislature passed a new law restoring their lands to them, but this did not make them Pennsylvanians. In 1786, an additional 250 families arrived from Connecticut, and a new militia of 600 men was formed to defend their homes from renewed attack by "Pennites."[16] The violence finally came to an end only when both states ratified the new Federal Constitution in 1788.

The tragedy of Vermont and Wyoming Valley is that individual Americans' sense of being American was not strong enough to overcome their sense of being a type of American. The separate states were closer to their hearts and lives and livelihoods and came first in their list of loyalties. Although their identity as Englishmen melted in the heat of the Revolutionary War, patriotic

Americans were not re-welded by that war into a united national sovereignty. As the war cooled, they hardened instead into separate state identities. It was only through the vehicle of state government that Americans would eventually develop the kind of sovereign national identity that would prevent further land disputes between individual states. The people of America did not accomplish nationality directly. It was we the states that ordained and established the American Constitution: The Preamble did not truly represent the ingenious process by which the nation was built.

But "We the people" sounded better than "We the states." It was good advertising of a good product — not a subterfuge. The union did become more perfect: justice, domestic tranquility, common defense, general welfare, and liberty were all established, insured, provided, promoted, and secured. The American nation became, through the Constitution, a sovereign political community commanding and deserving the primary loyalty of its citizens.

The ingenious mechanism by which this occurred had nothing to do with democracy or civil liberties. The new constitution allowed no more of either than already existed under state governments. *Democracy* was considered something of a dirty word by most influential men of the time, carrying connotations of mob rule and instability. It is not once mentioned in the Constitution. The right to vote, in terms of which democracy is usually defined, was left up to the states, most of which retained property qualifications both for voting and holding office. Civil liberties were not guaranteed by the Constitution as it was originally presented — they were added as amendments only after ratification. The real genius of the American Constitution was not freedom or popular rule but bicameral federalism.

The fundamental problem confronting the founding fathers at the Convention in Philadelphia was that the states were both equal and unequal and that both the equality and the inequality would have to be represented in the new system. The states would have to be recognized *as they were* in order to be welded together without heating them up again. Each state had to be incorporated into the new arrangement in ways that acknowledged the reality of its relation to the other states and to the individual people in all the states. As independent sovereign bodies, they were equal; as populations of American citizens, they were not. Some of the larger states had several times as many people as the smaller states.

The states were the true donors of sovereign power to the new system, but the people of each state were the ultimate source of sovereignty to the states. Legitimacy for the national government would be derived from its immediate predecessor and, at the same time, from its most fundamental constituency. The system had to provide for the gradual evolution of sovereignty away from the states and at the same time create a bridge of immediate sovereignty to the people. This was not easily accomplished and not immediately recognized at the Convention to be the central problem at hand.

James Madison arrived early in Philadelphia. While waiting for the Convention to assemble, he and a few other Virginians came up with a set of initial proposals that would not directly represent state governments in the new government. The legislature he proposed was bicameral, but both houses would be elected proportionally — that is, according to the number of people in each state. State governments would remain but they would not be represented in the central government at all, equally or otherwise. The central government would not derive its legitimacy from the states but from the people directly. This idea became identified as a *national* (as opposed to a *federal*) plan in that there would be no intermediary between the nation and the people and no clear status for states as creators of the central government. The Virginia Plan would benefit Virginia over other states because it was one of the more populous states and would send more representatives to the central government than the smaller states. It was, therefore, a plan that would recognize the inequality of the states without recognizing their equality.

This point was not lost on William Paterson of New Jersey. His response to the Virginia Plan was to propose a unicameral central government in which each state was equally represented regardless of its population. The New Jersey Plan would have been little more than a warmed-over Articles of Confederation because it called for no real transfer of power to the national government other than rights to regulate commerce, issue currency, and levy taxes. It recognized the equality of the states without recognizing their inequality.

Paterson probably did not expect the Convention to accept his plan as presented. More likely, he was putting the larger states on notice that the small states would not accept representation by population, and that the states would demand to live on in the new government, one way or another. It is interesting that, in some of his initial reactions to the Virginia Plan, he may have been trying to secure the survival of the states by scaring other delegates with the prospect of obliterating them altogether:

> resolved, that all the Lands contained within the Limits of each state individually, and to the U.S. generally be considered as constituting one Body or Mass, and be divided into thirteen or more integral parts.
>   Resolved, That such Divisions or integral Parts shall be styled Districts.[17]

Paterson's New Jersey colleague, Judge David Brearly, even suggested that, in order for a system like the Virginia Plan to be just, "a map of the U.S. be spread out, that all the existing boundaries be erased, and that a new partition of the whole be made into 13 equal parts."[18]

We will never know if Paterson and Brearly were truly serious, manipulating fears, or thinking off the top of their heads, but the overall effect of their plan was to recognize that the new government would have to be granted by existing state governments. If the transition of sovereignty were to be made peacefully, or made at all, it would have to be made from the starting point of power relations *as they were*. The new government was not going to be dreamed up without some relation to the existing order, James Madison notwithstanding.

But the Convention was to go through another scare before the real work of compromise would begin. Alexander Hamilton — who was the moving force behind the Convention and the most respected advocate of a strong central government — delivered a six-hour lecture to the assembly on the benefits of a constitutional monarchy. What America really needed to assure domestic tranquility and provide for the common defense, he said, was a king.

Presented with the extremes of hereditary autocracy and the annihilation of the states, members of the Convention knew the pressure was on to come up with something that would work. There was no set path ahead of them, and bridges behind them were beginning to burn. A compromise proposed at this point by the Connecticut delegation made sense to everyone: Why not allow direct state representation in one house of a bicameral federal legislature and popular representation in the other? This would create a central government that would incorporate existing sovereignties and at the same time reach the people directly without the intermediary of state government. It would be both equal and unequal in exactly the way the states were equal and unequal. Paterson, though his own plan had just been voted down, accepted the idea immediately. Madison, still attached to his strictly national idea, held out for the original Virginia Plan, and Hamilton, unused to compromise of any kind, gave up and left for New York.

The genius of the bicameral federalism proposed in the Connecticut Compromise was that it set up a new level of civil order that recognized the existing order and used existing patterns of custom, language, culture, and law enforcement. The same bicameral system can be applied on any level: local, national, or global. It allows for the evolution of centralized sovereignty in a deliberate, conscious, and gradual manner and establishes simultaneously the equal representation of existing sovereign entities and of individuals directly. Central authority is allowed to grow naturally, unabruptly, and flexibly — and within limits set by constituent states and individuals. Federal authority can be carefully delineated and restricted while allowed to seek its natural level of propriety. Creating a federal arrangement with a built-in tension between the new and old governments allows each succeeding generation room to interpret the original mandate.

Voting at the Convention was by state. State legislatures chose the delegates, instructed them, and insisted that they not exceed the authority given them. That authority was limited to amending the Articles of Confederation. The Convention became a revolution when delegates *did* exceed their authority by throwing out the Articles altogether. According to terms of the Articles, no changes could be made without unanimous consent of all thirteen states, but the ratification procedure outlined in the new Constitution allowed for the institution of the new system with the approval of only nine. The new Constitution was, therefore, illegal — and thereby revolutionary.

A clean break was made with the past. But each state would continue to exist as a separate, however subordinate, political entity with its prominence in the new system bearing some proportionality to that in the existing system. There would be no winners or losers. A common sacrifice would be borne by all; the states would experience a frightful hemorrhage of political power, but they would survive and live on in reduced form. The energies released would be gathered in by a new collective of the whole that would be greater than any of its parts separately or of all parts together, as they then were. America had found a body for its soul.

Bicameral federalism adapts a natural and necessary cleavage in the structure of legislative process to the bifurcated source of central authority itself. Even if a legislature does not constitute a federation, bicameralism is generally best because it establishes two separate legislative houses with approximately equal powers to protect the electorate from the dangers of fanaticism and demagoguery in either one of them. Most state legislatures, though not themselves federations, are bicameral for this reason. If the legislature does constitute a federation, the constituency of each house may be kept separate — one house representing an intermediate level of government and the other representing the people directly. In this way, bicameralism checks and balances authority within the legislature while at the same time protecting interests of the parts and of the whole. On a global level, the same structure can be adopted with one house of the legislature representing national governments and the other the people directly. (Executive authority, in the absence of foreign relations, may be much more limited than in a national government.)

The convention at Philadelphia, besides creating a stable and flexible government well suited to its environment, was unique in the manner in which it accomplished its goal. First, the scope and scale of the new system developed not from trial and tradition but from ideas. It was a conscious and deliberate application of thought to reality, a feat rarely accomplished in the business of establishing new government. Second, the transfer of sovereignty occurred without violence: There was no war of legitimacy between old and new governments, as is nearly always the case.

There is a relation, I believe, between these two. America was isolated, briefly, from external influences. The intermittent struggle for global influence between Britain and France — out of which America had snatched her independence a few years before and into which she would soon find herself re-embroiled — was at a temporary lull. There were no major armies or navies for thousands of miles. Internal factions had no recourse to external allies. She could afford to concentrate, for a few brief years, on what was best for her alone. Consideration could be given to conditions before they arose: how to prevent a president from becoming too powerful, how to pass a bill into law, how to devise a system for overriding vetoes. This was precious time for reflection; the future could be anticipated — America could sit and think things out. Not least of the things on her mind was how to keep the state governments happy — how to make those who would pay the greatest price satisfied with what they would buy. The creation of a sovereign federal government was nonviolent *because* it was conscious and deliberate.

There are those who would argue that the real transfer of sovereignty did not occur until the Civil War — that it was through the violence at Shiloh and Antietam that sovereignty moved once and for all from the states to the central government. They are right in that the question of ultimate sovereignty was answered with ink at Philadelphia and with blood at Gettysburg. But in the three generations between them, the federal government had time to show what it could do. It did not have to fight for its life during infancy, as do most new governments. The rational half of the American political psyche could be converted at one time and the other half later. If it were too much for any one man or generation to handle at once, the job could be divided; Madison and Hamilton would create in one age what Lincoln in his own age would preserve.

19. Carlisle, Pennsylvania

ON DECEMBER 26, 1787, A SMALL BAND OF SUPPORTERS OF the new United States Constitution attempted to stage a public demonstration at Carlisle, Pennsylvania, in the heart of the radical Cumberland Valley. They dragged a cannon onto the town square and prepared a bonfire. Opposition appeared spontaneously from all directions and a riot ensued. The Federalists were forced to withdraw, with injuries.

> I assure you it was laughable to see lawyers, doctors, colonels, etc., etc., leave the scene of their rejoicing in such haste, and run some one way and some another, so that in about three minutes from the first commencement of the battle, there was not one of the rejoicing party to be seen on the ground....[19]

The anti-Federalists took possession of the square and burned a copy of the Constitution. The next day the Federalists retook the square, with firearms. The anti-Federalists counter-demonstrated in the streets, burning effigies of Federalist leaders. The Federalists asked the Supreme Court of the state to issue arrest warrants for twenty of the anti-Federalist leaders as tensions mounted on both sides. Seven were arrested and the countryside rose up in arms against the Federalists.

> Immediately the country took to alarm hearing that a number of persons were confined in prison for opposing a measure that was intended to give sanction to the proposed Federal Constitution.[20]

The militia assembled on March 1, 1788, some one thousand to fifteen hundred men, and forced the local Federalist authorities to back down. The militia then marched to the jailhouse and freed the heroic seven.[21]

> And we are well convinced that nothing less than a full recantation and annihilation of the proposed aristocratic delusion will appease the insulted and enraged defenders of liberty.[22]

These were patriotic men. Those who rioted in the streets and those who rose up with the militia were all patriotic men. Many of them had served under Washington in the Revolutionary War. They were against the Federalists and against the Constitution, but they were not against America. But how could they have been so misguided as to take up arms against the very embodiment of the nation? How could they so fervently oppose our most sacred institution? If they were who we were at Lexington and Saratoga and Yorktown, how could they be so violently against what we have since become?

The rioters and militiamen of Carlisle had won a war for individual rights and for the local democracy of their state governments. They saw in the federal Constitution a move back toward a distant centralized authority. The war had established a tradition in the American countryside: When rights are threatened, you take the musket down from the mantelpiece and assemble with your neighbors at the courthouse. It had been a few years, but the men of Carlisle still knew how to do it. They were as prepared as ever to kill and die for freedom.

I believe that if the men of Carlisle could have seen the growth of the American republic around the Constitution of 1787 that they would not have opposed it. If they had known that the new federal system would become the true embodiment of the country they so loved, they would have supported it fully and in time come to honor and respect it the way we do. But they did not know that the Constitution would become who we are as a people. They had no idea that the newfangled system dreamed up by an urban conspiracy of wealthy lawyers and plantation owners would one day become the mechanism of American democracy. They did not understand what was happening. Somebody was taking away their rights and their local government, and they did not like what they saw. They were standing up for what they thought was right, and I respect them for that, but I believe they were dead wrong in opposing the formation of a sovereign central government for America. They might have spoiled it for everyone.

As there was opposition to the American Constitution in the 1780s, there will also be opposition to global unity in the coming years. Good people, loyal people, patriotic people will oppose any higher and more distant level of government. There will be rumors and conjectures of grand conspiracies. There will be confusion and misgivings. People will feel threatened. There will be many interpretations of what is happening and why. Most people will not understand what is happening and will oppose any system or idea or view of the world that limits or even questions national authority. Even those who see the practical necessity of unity will fear losing local and national control. Everyone will feel a threat to his or her individual rights.

What anti-Federalists feared most in 1787 was the loss of individual rights. There were other issues — the Federalists were generally rich, pro-commerce, antidemocratic, and against paper currency — but the main issue was rights. What about trial by jury; what about freedom of the press, freedom of speech and assembly, freedom of religion? What was to keep this new government from oppressing its people, taxing them to death, or locking them up? What was to keep it from being as bad as the British government?

The Founding Fathers did not think a Bill of Rights was necessary. Or if they did, they were too exhausted by the end of the summer in Philadelphia to bother writing one. But that's what the people who opposed the Constitution wanted most. They were less concerned with legislative process and the niceties of how to appoint ambassadors than with how this new government might affect them personally. They had fought for their rights, and they aimed to keep them. The Founding Fathers did not realize this. Intent on spelling out what the new government *would* be, they gave no thought to what it *would not* be. If it was created by and for the people, how could it possibly oppress them? Political oppression was something only monarchical governments could do. It was important to enumerate what a republican government could do, but why enumerate what it could not do? Wouldn't this be obvious? Hamilton thought that a Bill of Rights was not only unnecessary but actually dangerous: If you enumerate all the rights you can think of, you may be saying that the ones you can't think of don't exist. But the people wanted their rights spelled out.

The greatest fear in transition to unity will be loss of rights. The peoples of the world will not consent to be governed without a specific list of civil liberties recognized and guaranteed by any new government. It will have to include at least what is guaranteed now by national governments. A proposed global federation will have to embrace the principle of limited government and enumerate the specific means by which it will enforce protection of basic freedoms for both nations and individuals.

The greatest gift of unified government is peace. Those who were most worried about their rights in the 1780s could not have imagined the peace the new federal government would provide American states and individuals. Left to the enraged citizens of Carlisle, Pennsylvania, American history might have been otherwise. America might have been thirteen strong, independent, warring states. With the Constitution, we travel across town or across borders to neighboring states and we are with our own people. We are one people. As citizens of a strong, unified country, we enjoy peace and protection and should appreciate the gift that was given to us many years ago. We should appreciate also the peace we will provide future generations if we are able to forge new government to meet the needs of the twenty-first century.

Human nature cannot be changed and should not be changed. It is human organization that can — and should — be changed.

20. The Federalist Papers

Among the many objects to which a wise and free people find it necessary to direct their attention, that of providing for their "safety" seems to be the first. [John Jay, No. 3][23]

WHAT JOHN JAY MEANS BY *SAFETY* IS FREEDOM FROM THE fear of being killed by other people. The primary purpose of any government according to Jay — and just about anyone else — is to protect citizens from murder, either by their immediate neighbors or by other governments. The rest is secondary.

A good government is one that best performs this most basic of functions. One government, Jay contends, is better than many — because it will be stronger than many separate governments but also because separate governments tend to conflict with one another, often creating more violence than they suppress. He was, of course, speaking of a central government on the national level, but everything he said about the advantages of such a government applies on any other level, including the global level.

The Federalist Papers deal with the particulars of the federal government proposed by the Constitutional Convention of 1787, but the higher level of government in question is justified in terms of general human experience. Like the Declaration of Independence and the Constitution itself, the underlying meaning and purpose of the Federalist Papers applies at all times and in all places. Their historical significance transcends their particular moment in history. They are an intellectual exploration of the universal dynamic of higher political order as it pertains specifically to the creation of the American federal union.

America needs, according to the writers of the Federalist Papers, a strong central government to keep the states from fighting, because that is what independent states do if there is no central authority.

John Jay's, Alexander Hamilton's, and James Madison's arguments in the Federalist Papers — for a single sovereign government in the place of lesser competing governments — still apply to the world situation as they applied to the national situation at the time they were written. The proposed federal government of 1787 would provide better protection for commerce, better insurance against riots and terrorism, a more stable currency, etc., in the same way that a global government in the twenty-first century would provide better protection for labor and commerce, better insurance against terrorism, and a more stable world economy. There is no question that it would provide better protection from warfare between competing governments. An effective global government would be what Jay calls a "good government" in that it would provide better safety to its people than the existing system of international anarchy.

The Federalist Papers were written for New York City newspapers between October 1787 and the summer of 1788, as the state was considering ratification of the federal Constitution proposed by the Philadelphia Convention. The new Constitution, though it could have gone into effect with only nine states, would never have succeeded without New York's large population, strong economy, and central location. But ratification was less certain in New York than in any other major state. Governor George Clinton was against it, and a majority of delegates to the state ratification convention were also predisposed against it.

Sensing danger to the cause, Hamilton began a propaganda campaign that became the Federalist Papers. He solicited the help of Madison and Jay along the way. He appealed directly to the rational side of human nature, recognizing all the while its limited sway over the whole of human nature. America was in a unique position, he stated,

> to decide the important question, whether societies of men are really capable or not of establishing good government from reflection and choice, or whether they are forever destined to depend for their political constitutions on accident and force... But this is a thing more ardently to be wished than seriously to be expected. [Hamilton, No.1]

Hamilton wished it desperately. He, more than anyone else, fought for the principle of a strong central government. He was the moving force behind the calling of the Philadelphia Convention and the moving force behind the finished product — and especially for ratification in New York. But Hamilton was less concerned with the form of the new government than with its scope and reach. He was not in regular attendance at the Convention, his ideas were not taken seriously by other delegates, and virtually none of his suggestions made their way into what became the United States Constitution. He would leave to others questions of suffrage and the particulars of legislative process; what interested him most was political and commercial strength. That strength, he hoped, would come from a unified system of commercial laws and regulations sustained by a sound currency and a central bank, all supported by a strong national army and navy.

> A unity of commercial, as well as political, interests can only result from a unity of government. [Hamilton, No.11]

The key feature of the new system was that, unlike the Articles of Confederation, its authority would extend directly to the people. Rather than being a government of governments, it would embody the population itself:

we must extend the authority of the Union to the persons of
the citizens: the only proper objects of government. [Hamilton,
No.15]

Hamilton points out in this passage the key weakness of the
present-day United Nations in world affairs: that it is composed
of nations only and not of the people. It was created by national
governments and continues to serve the interests of national governments, often at the expense of the people. People do not vote
in the United Nations; they are not regulated or taxed by it directly,
and they feel no allegiance to it. It has little legitimacy in representing the interest of humanity as a whole and is kept deliberately weak by member nations, who have the most to lose by a
strong global government. Hamilton saw the need for the
American government to reach past the states to the people
directly, as he would no doubt see the need now for an effective
global government to reach past national governments to the
people themselves.

But the state governments would not disappear with the institution of the federal government, as James Madison states in Federalist Paper No. 14:

> In the first place it is to be remembered that the general gov-
> ernment is not to be charged with the whole power of making
> and administering laws. Its jurisdiction is limited to certain
> enumerated objects, which concern all the members of the
> republic, but which are not to be attained by the separate pro-
> visions of any. The subordinate governments, which can
> extend their care to all those other objects which can be sepa-
> rately provided for, will retain their due authority and activity.

Nor will national governments disappear with the arrival of
global unity. In either case, *sovereignty* moves to the central authority but the entirety of government does not. State governments to
this day are charged with the important matters of education,

infrastructure, and criminal law within the American federal system, and national governments will continue to govern purely internal matters within any properly instituted global system. The difference under unity will be a clear voice for the interests of the world as a whole (the way there is now a voice for America as a whole) and the suppression of international warfare. Iraq will no longer have the right to invade Kuwait, nor America Iraq, the way New York no longer has the right to invade Vermont or Connecticut to invade Pennsylvania. The exact relation between central and subordinate governments cannot be determined in advance and will no doubt shift over time. But with flexibility built into the system, power-sharing arrangements will be worked out in time:

> happily for the "republican cause", the practicable sphere may
> be carried to a very great extent by a judicious modification
> and mixture of the "federal principle." [Madison, No.51]

Madison opposed the federal principle at the Convention, holding out for his "national" principle to the last minute. But he finally gave in to it and became fully convinced of it by the time he began contributing to the Federalist Papers. Ironically, he eventually became known as the "father" of the federal Constitution. Hamilton, who opposed democratic rule categorically and would have preferred a constitutional monarchy to the Philadelphia product in any case, also adopted and argued for the federal principle in the Federalist Papers and became the leading champion of the Federalist cause. It is largely due to the influence of these men that the New York convention finally voted by a narrow majority in favor of the Constitution, and it is due to that victory that the Constitution eventually went into effect in all thirteen states.

The big winners of the Federalist era were not those who won particular battles, but those who, like Madison and Hamilton, kept their eyes on the big picture — those who lost the battles but won the war. Both would eloquently defend particulars of the new constitutional arrangement that they had not supported (and in some cases vehemently opposed at the convention). It is safe to say that each was transformed by his experience in Philadelphia and that each perhaps convinced himself to some extent through the process of writing the Federalist Papers. Each loved his country and good government more than he loved his own ideas.

We can expect that, in a similar manner, when it comes time to draw out the specifics of global government, those who fight to the end for their own ideas may not be the real winners. Those who keep the big picture in front of them and listen carefully will come away with the prize. The real heroes will be those who are convinced in the process itself. The specifics will determine the character and the popularity of the new system, but the underlying issue will always return, as it did in 1788, to the question of *safety*. We need protection from weapons of mass destruction by eliminating divisions in the human family that make those weapons seem necessary.

> Safety from external danger is the most powerful director of national conduct. Even the ardent love of liberty will, after a time, give way to its dictates. [Hamilton, No.8])

And safety comes from unity:

> As the safety of the whole is the interest of the whole, and cannot be provided for without government, either one or more or many, let us inquire whether one good government is not, relative to the object in question, more competent than any other given number whatever. [Jay, No. 4]

Jay wrote of one government. He meant, of course, one government for America: one sovereign national government instead of many competing state governments. But the "one government" of the globalist era will be truly one government. There will be no other governments with which it will compete. It will provide better safety than the existing system of competing national governments by virtue of being global. As with any government, it will provide safety from within; but unlike any other government, it will not have to provide safety from without because there will be no without. There will be no international war. Not only will there be no war, there will be no *possibility* of war. War will become a structural impossibility. The thought of one nation invading another in the twenty-first century will become as absurd as the thought of one American state invading another in the twentieth. The larger government in either case will not allow it.

The absence of *war* means avoiding nuclear annihilation; the absence of the *possibility of war* means an enormous savings in defense expenditures. A minimum level of force will be necessary to maintain security, but there will be no need for standing armies or large defense establishments. There will be no need for nations to defend themselves. This will create a tidal wave of new wealth for health care, education, infrastructure, environmental protection, economic development, space exploration, and alternative energy development. The world will have to find other uses for the nearly one trillion dollars it now spends each year preparing to kill people.

Jay foresaw in his quest for a strong central government the powerful army and navy that America now has. (I will not give him credit for the air force.) But if his real motive was safety and not power for its own sake, he would have to admit that in today's world we would do better without them. They endanger America's safety more than they ensure it. If, instead of relying on our ability to threaten other people with war, we follow Jay's advice and adopt one government, as opposed to any other given number whatever, we will ensure a better chance at "good" government — that is, at a government that will provide true safety in the current situation. Like Jay and Hamilton and Madison in their time, we will construct a system that provides safety through a larger and more inclusive structure. Our new system will have all the advantages of theirs and will have one that theirs does not have: It will not have to defend itself from other such systems. It will not have to prepare to kill massive numbers of people in order to be "good." In its oneness it will provide safety by eliminating the divisions in human civilization that lead to war.

21. Gettysburg

Four score and seven years ago our fathers brought forth upon
this continent, a new nation, conceived in Liberty, and dedicated to the proposition that all men are created equal.

Now we are engaged in a great civil war, testing whether
that nation, or any nation so conceived and so dedicated, can
long endure...

...that this nation, under God, shall have a new birth of
freedom — and that government of the people, by the people,
for the people, shall not perish from the earth.

— *Abraham Lincoln*

ONE THOUSAND, SEVEN HUNDRED SEVENTY-SIX FROM ONE
thousand eight hundred sixty-three is eighty-seven. But he did not
say "eighty-seven" years — he said "four score and seven." It is
not a rhyme; the number is not special and has no meaning that
can be related to some other truth. There is no reason to start a
speech with a number in any case, much less a number whose
value is shrouded in archaic usage. He might more easily have
said, "Our fathers started this country eighty-seven years ago..."

But "Four score and seven" sounds plain good. It is poetry.
The world does, in fact, long remember what Lincoln said —
because it sounds good. It has a ring that has lasted through the
ages. And the idea embodied in the Gettysburg Address has also
lasted partly because it was so poetically expressed.

The idea itself is not especially interesting. It is far less creative than the original founding of the American republic, and

certainly not poetic, but it is every bit as important. The idea is *context* of majority rule. People know the speech because of its poetry, but few understand the idea embodied in the Gettysburg Address.

The speech and the war were about the right of a majority to impose its will on a minority — not about slavery, or equality, or civil rights. These were the immediate issues that brought about the crisis, but the crisis centered on the question of *context*.

Lincoln represented the majority: The North consisted at that time of twenty-four of the thirty-five states and about seventy-one percent of the total population. He was elected in 1860 *entirely by Northern votes*: not a single electoral vote went for him in any Southern state. He was not even on the ballot in some of them. Yet he was president of *all* the states — or claimed to be. He claimed that the *context* of his majority included the minority, willing or not.

As the votes were cast for Lincoln's election, the South Carolina legislature remained in session through the night. When it was clear that a man receiving all of his votes from the North would preside over them, they seceded from the Union. The Union no longer represented *them*. They did not dispute the election or Lincoln's right to represent the North, nor did they dispute the principle of majority rule. They disputed only the context within which it was expressed. They wanted a new context in which they would themselves be a majority. They wanted self-government, and the right to define *self*, the same sorts of things that independence movements everywhere want, including our own such movement, eighty-some years before.

But to Lincoln, majority rule and the context of majority rule were inseparable. Majority rule makes sense only if its context is perpetual. If the minority can drop out whenever it does not like the outcome of a particular decision, nothing will ever be decided. Popular government will become an absurdity. If two or three counties of South Carolina do not approve of what is going on in

Charleston and decide to leave the state and set up their own government, what is left of South Carolina? And what if some districts or individuals of those counties decide to go their own way? What, then, is left of any government? The context of a majority is, therefore, according to Lincoln, government itself. There is no majority unless there is also a minority.

More than forty thousand Americans lay dead or dying on the field at Gettysburg, a field small enough to shout across. It was the greatest battle of the Civil War and of American history. If asked what they were fighting for, few men there would have said anything about a "context for majority rule" or any other fine point of political philosophy. But that is why they were there. They gave their last full measure of devotion not for freedom or equality but for the Union, the context within which they could decide for, or against, freedom or equality. They fought not for democracy, but for the structure within which it would make sense. They were testing whether a nation conceived in liberty and dedicated to the principle of majority rule could long maintain its context. And what if it could not? What if the determined minority, newly conceived and stubborn in defense of its rights and independence, were to prevail? What if the South were to win? Would the idea of popular government be ruined?

For Lincoln, the test at Gettysburg was not of Americans but of human beings everywhere. He did not say "in this country" but "upon this continent." The image is of the earth itself, with one of its several continents at center stage. The actors are North American, but the audience is European, African, South American, and Asian. The action revolves around the great question of whether the featured nation, dedicated as it is to the principle of human equality — *or any nation* so conceived and so dedicated — can actually decide things and do them.

If it can, mankind has a model that it may build from. If not, there will be no second chance. Popular government will have failed.

But for Lincoln, what is the context for majority rule once the earth and not one of its continents becomes the stage and those in the audience become actors? What then of the Union that he fought so hard to preserve? Does he preserve it against absorption as well as dissolution, against global integration as well as against sectional disintegration? He could not, of course, ask this question, much less answer it, and we are just as grateful. We do not, in fact, need Lincoln just now. He might prove embarrassing. What we need now are Jefferson and Madison and even, I will say, Hamilton. We need what they brought forth three score and fifteen years before Gettysburg.

We will need Lincoln later, when some, in search of freedom, threaten to undo what has been done. Then we will hear his honored dead speaking in particulars. Only then will the liberty we conceive, once born, have the chance to perish forever.

Part V — The Possible

.

22. The Enemy

WHEN THE EARTH IS YOUR CONCERN, GOODNESS WILL bounce off the ends of the universe. It will not thin with distance. The oceans will no longer drown you; gravity will contain the continents. There will be closure and no limit to your love; the world will be the sphere of operations. No one will be too far away. When the earth is your concern, there will be no enemy, and the enemy will choose you.

From vision there is thought, from thought belief, and from belief, the enemy. Wholeness will divide the universe. A thought, on becoming action, reduces to dimensional form; it is incomplete and always wrong. It does not fit in the world. Creating itself, it creates its opposite, setting one against another. This is where compassion leads. There is nothing more dangerous than compassion — and nothing better. Doing for others is the ultimate good, but there is no concept of Man on Earth that men and women share. There is no one good thing to do. Love makes enemies that need us.

The enemy is kind, cruel, evil, compassionate, strong, brave, timid. He hates you, smiling, thinking. He turns, looking at you, trying to find a way in. Your life does not matter to him. Your day does not matter. Your ideas do not matter. Your mother holding you to her breast does not matter. He has forgotten. Pointing, he overruns you, rushing, shouting, planting his flag, waving, cheered by his friends, standing over you, watching you think your last thoughts, the universe fading, thinking only his.

He hates you. You are his redcoat, his gook, his Wasichu hiding naked in the grass when the battle is lost, tormented and killed by his women.

He will fool you, divert you, take what you have done and turn it to his own. He will deceive your friends and undermine their trust. He will keep a distance, sleep when you are sleeping, wake when you are waking, wake while you are sleeping, and strike. He is stronger than you, or weaker. He hates what you stand for but sees you behind your face.

You are misled, wrong, dangerous, evil. But you are within his concern; he prays for you. You will never understand him; he is there because you believe and do not see. You will fight, struggle, kick, scream, and strain until you become him. He will tear at your face until you become him.

Without the enemy there is no belief. He defines who we are and gives meaning to what we do. We owe commitment to him and create ourselves in the image of his reflected love.

The enemy loves himself, his country, and his family. He believes in God or does not. His friends admire him for his intellect and willingness to sacrifice for everyone, for them, and that is why he does it. In his mind, there are things worth fighting for and worth fighting against, and he will never understand you. He wants to do for more than himself. He has saved us in the past.

He will kill you; there is nothing we can do about that.

Robert McNamara, secretary of defense under presidents Kennedy and Johnson, said that we should empathize with the enemy. Empathize, not sympathize — not take on his feelings as our own, but at least know what they are — put ourselves in his shoes. No matter how horrible he may be and how much he may wish to kill us, we should know what he wants.

McNamara knew what he was talking about. He had a well-developed concept of enemy. In World War II, he served in the Air Force Office of Statistical Control, planning and assessing bombing raids over Japan. The American B-29 bomber had just been developed for high-altitude missions above the danger of enemy fighter planes and antiaircraft fire. At 23,000 feet, it could deliver a load of thousand-pound explosives over enemy targets and return to its base in relative safety. But despite increased safety for the crew, altitude came at the expense of accuracy. Important targets were missed, and unimportant nontargets hit. So McNamara came up with the idea of flying in at 5,000 feet and using incendiary bombs. More planes were lost, but much greater damage accomplished. In one night mission in March 1945, fifty square miles of Tokyo was destroyed and 100,000 Japanese civilians burned to death — more than were killed later that summer in Hiroshima or Nagasaki.

McNamara's concept of enemy matured when he served as secretary of defense. Under Kennedy, he helped develop a response to Khrushchev's placement of nuclear weapons in Cuba. Also under Kennedy and later under Johnson, he managed the American war in Vietnam. It was in these situations (where he was shaping military policy) that he learned the importance of empathy. In Cuba he knew what the enemy wanted and was able to avoid nuclear war; in Vietnam he did not know what the enemy wanted and fought a war that need not have been fought.

In October 1962, there were 162 nuclear weapons in Cuba deployed in Russian missiles aimed at ninety million American civilians from Florida to Washington, D.C. Khrushchev claimed that Russia was producing home-based intercontinental missiles "like sausages" and that he would "bury" us. When American intelligence discovered the missiles in Cuba, 180,000 American soldiers were mobilized for war, and B-52 strategic bombers were placed on red alert for possible attacks on targets in Cuba and Russia.

President Kennedy met with advisers to decide whether Cuba was worth an all-out nuclear confrontation. McNamara tried to come up with a strategy that would avoid the worst. General Curtis LeMay, McNamara's commanding officer during World War II, wanted to blow Cuba off the map. It was his feeling that nuclear war with Russia was inevitable and that it was better fought now, while the United States held a strategic advantage. Kennedy thought there was no way to negotiate the missiles out of Cuba and that Khrushchev would never back down without a fight. But Tommy Thompson, former ambassador to Moscow, disagreed. He and his wife had spent a considerable amount of time with the Soviet leader and knew that Khrushchev did not want a nuclear confrontation. What he wanted was to be seen defending Cuba against U.S. aggression. After all, the U.S. had sponsored the Bay of Pigs invasion of Cuba two years earlier. If he could say to his people that he had saved Cuba from America, he would be in a position to back down. Kennedy considered what Thompson said and decided to give it a try. He offered a public pledge of non-aggression against Cuba and the withdrawal of American missiles in Turkey in exchange for the withdrawal of Russian missiles from Cuba. As Thompson foresaw, Khrushchev accepted the offer and nuclear war was averted. Knowing the enemy literally saved the world. (General LeMay was horribly disappointed.)

In the case of Vietnam, McNamara admitted that he did not know the enemy. For him, the context was the Cold War: Communist North Vietnam invading free South Vietnam, backed and supplied by Communist Russia and Communist China. Fifty-eight thousand Americans died fighting for freedom. Two to three times as many bombs were dropped on Vietnam as in Europe during all of World War II.

For the Vietnamese, the context of the war was anticolonialism. Before World War II, they spent years fighting French colonialism. During the war they spent years fighting Japanese colonialism. After the war they spent more years fighting the French again. Ho Chi Minh, educated in Europe and aware of America's own anticolonial history, asked the United States for aid against the French. He was a Communist, but at the Vietnamese independence ceremonies following the final defeat of the French, he quoted from the American Declaration of Independence. Ho did not know that the United States, despite its own history, was far more interested in fighting Communism than fighting colonialism. The U.S. had been supplying the French against him since the Communist takeover of China in 1949, and in 1954, with the defeat of the French at Dien Bien Phu, the U.S. took up the war against Ho where the French left off.

According to the Geneva Conference ending the war with the French, the southern portion of the country was to be administered separately from the north until elections could be held in 1956 to form a unified national government. Ngo Dinh Diem, an anti-Communist leader with strong U.S. support, arose in the south but soon met armed resistance from Communist followers of Ho known as the Vietcong.

Diem suspended local elections in the south and convinced the Eisenhower administration that national elections would not be fairly administered. When it became clear that Ho Chi Minh would win easily in both north and south, Diem and the United States postponed the elections indefinitely and set up a separate South Vietnamese government. From the Vietnamese perspective, what followed was a civil war. At least 3,400,000 of them died.

Two separate wars were thus fought at the same time and in the same place. Neither side understood what the other wanted.

Many years later, McNamara met in Hanoi with the former Vietnamese foreign minister and was told that the Vietnamese were convinced that America wanted to enslave them as had France and Japan. When told that all they wanted was independence from France, Japan, America, China, and everyone else, McNamara said, "Oh, we would have given you that."

When McNamara explained to the former minister that what America wanted was to prevent the spread of a monolithic world communism from Russia and China through Vietnam and the rest of Southeast Asia, the minister responded that Vietnam would never be and had never been a pawn of Russia or China. "We have been fighting China for a thousand years," he added.

Nobody knew.

When Al Qaeda attacked the United States in September 2001, everybody wondered how anyone could hate America so much. No one knew what the terrorists wanted or how they expected to get it by killing thousands of innocent American and international civilians going about their daily lives. We did not know what it was like to be an Arab, without an army, standing on the shores of the Persian Gulf watching American jets flying overhead and American ships unloading troops on holy soil. We did not know what it was like for Arab parents to keep their teenage daughters away from American movies and magazines and televised half-time shows at the Super Bowl. There was no sympathy in our hearts and no empathy in our minds for those who did not accept our way of life in their midst, and there was no willingness to imagine what it would be like to have *their* way of life in *our* midst. There was no attempt to see things from their point of view.

We did not know that Al Qaeda was formed not in Iraq or Iran or Syria or Palestine, but in Saudi Arabia, one of our closest allies, and that what Osama Bin Laden wanted was the removal of American troops from the Persian Gulf. He wanted Arabs, not infidel Americans, to expel Saddam Hussein from Kuwait. He was proud of being an Arab and a Muslim. He wanted to revive the spirit of Islam in a holy war against the West. We did not understand that he and Saddam were enemies and that Al Qaeda was the last thing Saddam wanted in Iraq.

We did not empathize for fear of sympathizing. We wanted revenge for September 11, but we did not know who the enemy was, so we imagined him and gave him imaginary mushroom clouds and imaginary chemical and biological weapons — and an imaginary connection to Al Qaeda. When these vanished in the light of day, we changed the reason for the war. Hatred is a powerful and creative force: An embarrassing number of Americans still think that Saddam Hussein was behind the attacks of September 11.

Who is the enemy in the "War on Terrorism"? What does he want? He is a vicious killer, we know, but is he anyone who uses violence against innocent civilians, at any altitude? Must he lack a conventional army? Our thinking stops at the label "terrorist." Why do they hate us? How can we see ourselves as we are seen? Why does support of occupying forces in Palestine, a war in Afghanistan, and two wars in Iraq look like a holy war against Islam? By acting as the enemy they would have us be, we are giving them the war they want and creating terrorist followers faster than we can kill them. Osama Bin Laden is directing American foreign policy. We do not have to give him what he wants to know what he wants, but we have to know what he wants to deal with him wisely.

McNamara also said that mistakes are inevitable and can be learned from most of the time. In the case of Vietnam, hindsight teaches what might have been done. In the case of the Cuban Missile Crisis, however, hindsight would have done no good at all. There would have been no hindsight. Mistakes in a major nuclear crisis, no matter how inevitable, are not allowed. There is only foresight.

I believe in one world — a world where all people are united politically and spiritually. Humanity runs deeper than race, culture, and nationality, and it is only upon humanity that we may build.

There is no one who is not us. This, I believe, is a great truth that overrides all other current considerations and will underlie any continuing civilization that we may have. A great truth bears the fruit of its logic: Anyone who does not understand this is wrong; anyone who opposes it is an enemy.

Now, I know that I am right because the earth is not large enough for political division in an age of intercontinental weaponry. Political division means war between nations, and war between nations will be nuclear and worse in the coming years. There is no way that it will not be. We are fortunate that the major nations are not currently aligned for war, but they were very close to war in the recent past and will be close to it again any number of times in the future. I do not know which nations will have the war, or if they will be nations, or how bad the war will be, but I do know that it will happen. I know it. Global unity will not be realized in time to avert this war, but it is likely to be realized soon afterward. This is all plain to me. It is logical and sufficiently vague to be accurate as a whole. I do not see why everyone else does not believe it.

The enemy believes that governments cause war and that the last thing we need is another layer of government. A world government, he believes, would be remote, inept, oppressive, and dictatorial. It would take away our rights as individuals and Americans. It would take away our national sovereignty, and we would be under the rule of foreigners. That which defines us most would no longer exist. This is worth fighting against. The enemy of globalism does not fight for the right of nations to have nuclear wars — he fights for what is right, and he is right.

But I will say that you must kill no man. You must see beyond him who opposes you. You must have no enemy. If there is human progress, it lies in that portion of our actions that do not cancel the actions of others.

> We are all republicans — we are all federalists. If there be any among us who would wish to dissolve this Union or to change its republican form, let them stand undisturbed as monuments of the safety with which error of opinion may be tolerated where reason is left free to combat it.
> — *Thomas Jefferson, First Inaugural, 1801*

23. Douglass Loop

A FEW WEEKS AFTER THE MAIN PART OF THE WAR WAS OVER we held another vigil at Douglass Loop. We were not sure what we were about or what the vigil was going to be about, so there was no central message. It was easy to know what to be against while the war was on, but we were not sure what to be for now that it seemed to be over.

We stood there for an hour. I had a few ideas for a sign but never got around to making one. There were too many ideas running through my head and not enough time to find poster board and the right kind of markers. We used to use old Anne Northup campaign posters, but they were gone now, all used up for yard signs in front of our houses.

Rooting around the garage earlier that day, I had found a world flag that someone had given me. In a shoebox below a shelf full of brushes and paint cans, I found an American flag of the same size. I had never done anything with either of them, never having been much of a flag person. They were both in good shape, their colors bright and unfaded, and I got to thinking. There was a twelve-foot length of plastic pipe on the floor by the wall, and with a drill and a piece of clothesline I soon had a pole with both flags flying high in the afternoon breeze — the world flag above the American. That really said something and said it without words. I cut the pole in half to fit in my car and put a coupling on one end so I could reassemble it. Now here I was, on the street again, my priorities on display to a candid world.

There were a few comments from passersby but mostly from my comrades, and the flagpole didn't seem to offend anyone. If it did, they drove on. It might have made some people think — you never know — but I was a little disappointed in the apparent lack of reaction. Didn't anybody see that the American flag wasn't on top, where it always belongs? Isn't there some kind of law or regulation against anything above the American flag?

I'd love to go to jail for this. Maybe we could get it on camera. The headlines would be: "Man Arrested for Putting World Over America." As if you could have America without a world to have it in, and there I would be, in handcuffs, proudly sacrificing myself to the greater cause.

But people just drove by. The reactions overall were about what they were before and during the war: about 20 percent honk and wave, often with the familiar two-finger V sign of peace, and about 10 percent give us a thumbs down or the familiar middle finger of war. (This seems to be the universally accepted mark of true patriotism.) The rest just drive by with blank expressions, as if thinking "Whaaat?" Once somebody stopped and said, "You mean the war in Iraq? What's that got to do with Douglass Loop?"

As the hour was coming to an end and I was getting ready to disassemble the pole, a car heading north on Bardstown Road came to a stop in the left lane. The driver rolled the window down. I could tell he was frustrated. Not mad, not violent, not even offended, just frustrated. He had no idea what to say but had to say something, his hand waving backward through the open window, as if addressing the thirty or so of us standing on the curb and dismissing us at the same time. "Why," he said as the traffic began backing up behind him. "Why do you people hate America?"

Normally, I do not respond to taunts or challenges in public demonstrations. The street is not a good place for rational discourse. But he was looking right at me as I stood on the curb holding the pole. There was no hatred in his face, as we often see in the superpatriots. He just could not believe what he was looking at. "We don't hate America," I shouted across two lanes of traffic. "Look, I'm flying the American flag!"

He started to say something, but somebody in the seat next to him gestured, and there was a honk behind him. The window rolled up and the car drove off. "What a jerk," someone behind me said.

We were heading back from dinner at Burt and Rosalyn's house, and there was this demonstration where Douglass Boulevard crosses Bardstown Road. I'd seen them there before, but they apparently hadn't heard that the war was over. I'm all for free speech, and thank God we live in a country where they can do that sort of thing, but what the hell were they protesting now? They must have been real disappointed that their own side won. Did they have any concept of the fact that young men and women were having to fight to protect their right to protest? Let 'em protest, I thought, I don't care. Shows how much freedom we really do have here. But do you think any of them would lift a finger to fight for their own freedom? I doubt it. They've always known it and take it for granted.

I was a little perturbed because my wife's nephew is over there. He's stationed in Qatar and wasn't in Iraq for the war, but we're all pretty concerned about him. They could send his unit in anytime. He's not in danger now, but just knowing somebody over there gives you a better sense of the reality of the situation. It's not just something in the news — it's real people whose lives are on the line. A piece of you is there. It's not just a topic of discussion. So I couldn't drive by a bunch of protesters and let them have the final word. I knew they all have their opinions about this and that, but this is not just an opinion to me. I've got people over there.

The other reason I was so put off was that Burt, my wife's father, was in World War II. We were talking about the war over dinner. He was a POW and had a hard time of it. He doesn't talk about it much, but the topic came up and I learned some things I didn't know before. It's amazing he survived at all.

He was sent to North Africa in 1943. His unit crossed to Sicily and landed in Italy a few weeks later. He saw a lot of fierce fighting somewhere near Monte Casino. His entire unit was surrounded and captured, and they spent almost a year in a German prison camp. The first thing the Germans did was find out who the Jews were in Burt's unit and separate them from the others. The Americans told the Germans they didn't know who was Jewish, and that they were all Americans and it didn't matter to them what their religion was. But the Germans had their ways. They keep bugging them about it, and they beat up Burt's commanding officer more than once. They took some guys away, but nobody knew if they were really Jewish or not. They never saw those guys again but heard that they ended up in a labor camp. Most of them probably died.

Things weren't much better for the rest of them. As the Germans began losing the war, the food got worse and worse. Usually they had thin half-rotten potato soup and a small piece of moldy bread. A lot of guys got sick and some of them died. They never had enough blankets and ran out of fuel over winter. They were cold and sick and hungry, and they said the worst part was that they didn't know what was happening. They heard rumors, but they never knew if the war would ever end or if they would ever get out. A lot of them gave up hope, and those were the guys who didn't make it. A lot of the guys who didn't have somebody waiting for them at home were the ones who didn't make it.

Toward the end of the war, as the German armies retreated, the camp was shut down, and what was left of Burt's unit was forced to march to another location. It was cold and they could barely walk, and the Germans were shooting people who couldn't keep up. They had to march all day long in the cold and were given little rest.

One time they came to a place along the road near a railroad track where the Germans had recently killed several hundred people, Jews or Poles. The blood was barely dried. A long ditch had been dug, probably by the victims themselves, but it hadn't been filled over. It must have been a rush job. Bodies were lying everywhere — all men, as far as he could tell. They were wearing striped uniforms — not the kind used by military prisoners — and they were all so thin their bones showed through their skin. He said it looked as if they would have died of hunger if they hadn't been shot. But the unit had to keep marching, so they kept on. Nobody said anything. Many of the guys said later that they would have gotten sick, but they couldn't afford to. They couldn't think about all those people; they had to think about themselves. It wouldn't have done any good to do anything else.

A few days later, they came close to the American lines. There was a lot of confusion, and the German guards melted away into the woods. There was firing back and forth, and the unit was afraid to come out in the open until the fighting calmed down. Burt said he was looking down a road while they were hiding and saw a tank coming toward them with an American flag. As it rolled by he choked and felt tears come to his eyes. He wanted to run out into the road but thought better of it. They were rescued later that day and fed. He said he never smoked a cigarette before that day or since, but a GI gave him one and he smoked it. Made him sick, but the guy really wanted him to have it.

That's what the flag means to Burt. And to Rosalyn, too. They didn't know each other until after the war, but she said that everybody at home pulled together during the war. Everybody was working for the same thing. She was making straps for parachute packs, and all her friends were working, too. The whole country had a purpose, people gave up a lot of comforts, and eventually we won. We didn't want to fight but we had to and we won. If *we hadn't stood up to Hitler, God knows what would have hap-pened.*

So we were driving back along Bardstown Road and I saw these people carrying signs and protesting against the war. They probably didn't think of themselves as on Saddam's side, but that's the effect they are having. They are Saddam's only chance now. If they keep protesting and he keeps picking off one American boy a day, he's hoping he can scare us out of there and bring back the good old days.

I've seen American flags with some of the protesters, but I don't think they know what it means. They don't appreciate it. They've never had to give up anything for it. They think the flag is some kind of joke. One guy had another flag flying above it, just to be in your face about it. They just don't know how good they have it. So I gave 'em a piece of my mind. Felt like saying more.

24. The Sons of Liberty

THE SONS OF LIBERTY DID NOT INVENT MOB VIOLENCE; what they invented was mob *rule*. Rioting and lawlessness was a tradition in America long before the Revolutionary War; what the Sons of Liberty did in the 1760s and 1770s was organize and channel it toward longer-range political goals. Members of the Sons of Liberty in Boston encouraged and instigated urban riots against British rule, but more important, they used lawlessness to keep themselves in control of local government and at the helm of the revolutionary movement.

Rioters in Colonial America were mostly workers, shopkeepers, young toughs, small merchants, blacks, beggars, and schoolboys. On November 5, 1764, there was a street war between rival South End and North End gangs in Boston involving a thousand or so people. This was a tradition in Boston and occurred every November 5, unless it fell on a Sunday, in which case the riot was postponed for a day.

This particular year, one person was killed and several more wounded, which was about normal. What was abnormal was that it was also the year the Stamp Act was proposed in Parliament. The leader of the South End gang, a mob chieftain and shoemaker by the name of Ebenezer Mackintosh, caught the attention of a secret group of Bostonians trying to organize political and economic resistance against the upcoming stamp taxes. The secret group called itself the "Loyal Nine," and included such notables as James Otis, John Avery, Thomas Dawes, and Sam Adams, most of them Harvard graduates and unlikely associates of Boston street thugs. Most of their activities to this point involved letter writing and forming an association among local merchants pledging to refrain from buying or consuming British goods. But members of the Nine were coming to realize that a boycott association was not going to be enough to stop the British Parliament. They would need a more direct means of confronting the new taxes, and they saw what they needed in Ebenezer Mackintosh.

Sam Adams, master of behind-the-scenes power brokering, managed to form an alliance between Mackintosh's South End toughs and the North End gang under Henry Swift. Henceforth, the two gangs, instead of fighting each other, would work together against the British under the control of Adams and the Loyal Nine. The two gang leaders were from then on often seen together on the streets. Meanwhile the Nine began regular, systematic correspondence with at least fifteen other revolutionary anti-Stamp Act cells in New York, New Haven, Newport, New London, Norwich, Charles Town, Annapolis, Portsmouth, and Albany. A sympathizer in the British Parliament, Colonel Isaac Barre, referred to them collectively in a Parliamentary speech as the "Sons of Liberty," and the name stuck.

The Sons in Boston did as much and more to control mobs as it did to incite them. By giving Mackintosh the post of "sealer of the leather" at the Boston town meeting, they insured his loyalty to their goals. Mackintosh, in turn, wielded discipline over his men. On one occasion, according to Peter Oliver, he

> paraded the Town with a Mob of 2000 Men in two Files, & passed by the Stadhouse, when the general Assembly were sitting, to display his Power: if a Whisper was heard among his Followers, the holding up of his Finger hushed it in a Moment: & when he had fully displayed his Authority, he marched his Men to the first Rendevouz, & Order'd them to retire peaceably to their several Homes; & was punctually obeyed.[24]

The Boston mob used the same single tactic over and over again: intimidation. They armed themselves with sticks, clubs, rocks, and tar and feathers, but not with firearms. It was illegal to discharge a firearm in the city of Boston, and this law was for the most part respected. They kicked, hit, threw, shattered, broke, burned, damaged, injured, maimed, and destroyed, but generally did not kill. Under the leadership of Adams and the Sons of Liberty, their target became not the city government or the colonial assembly, but the British Crown and its direct representatives in Boston.

When Andrew Oliver was appointed stamp distributor for the new tax, the mob tore his house to pieces, hanged him in effigy, and forced him to resign. Parliament now had no practical means of enforcing the Stamp Act.

The tactic worked so well that its success was immediately relayed to other colonies. Within weeks every stamp distributor in every colony except Georgia was intimidated by organized mobs and forced to resign his post. Later, the Boston mob attacked the houses of the customs surveyor and the comptroller and the Custom House and admiralty offices. When this was not enough, they turned on the Lieutenant-Governor of Massachusetts, Thomas Hutchinson, and destroyed his house. These were all carefully selected targets with a clear political message.

Sam Adams and other core members of the Sons of Liberty, if they took any direct part at all in these actions, dressed in workmen's clothes and avoided recognition. If things went too far, as they did in the case of Hutchinson's house, the leadership often publicly repudiated the excesses of mob violence that they had themselves planned.

There was no regular, modern-style police force in Boston at the time; if there had been, the American Revolution, if it could have happened at all, would have happened very differently. There was a sheriff and a few justices of the peace but no regular body of officers trained and ready to prevent lawlessness on a scale involving more than one or two people. The colonial governor was constantly pleading with the sheriff and justices to do their jobs, but what can three or four men do in the face of hundreds of angry and unpredictable people? The crowd could very well turn on *them*. After the destruction of Hutchinson's house, local authorities did manage to round up a half dozen or so that they could identify as having taken part. But another mob showed up at the jailer's and threaten to destroy *his house* until he surrendered the keys to the jail.

The only measure the British government could take to control the mob and to enforce Parliamentary laws was to send in regular troops. But even redcoats could not control the crowds. Military officers were not legally empowered in civilian affairs, having to be called to act by a civil authority — in this case the Colonial government. But the Sons of Liberty controlled the Boston town meeting, and Sam Adams controlled the Colonial Assembly through his position as clerk.

The Colonial governor was so intimidated by the mob that he never openly admitted to asking British authorities for the troops and would never risk publicly calling them into action. So they stayed on, quartered in public buildings, living at public expense, resented and hated by those they were supposed to be protecting. Boston was not an official outpost of Colonial military administration, and there was no current war with the French, the Spanish, or the Indians. The troops could have only one purpose: to suppress American liberty.

British troops also competed with American colonials for jobs. They were allowed to supplement meager military wages with part-time employment in their spare time. Private Patrick Walker of the 29th Regiment appeared outside a ropeworks on March 2, 1770, asking for a job. A rope maker by the name of William Green, standing with a few of his fellow workers, suggested the soldier could go clean out the latrine. Walker responded by suggesting Green could go clean it himself, and a fight ensued.

Outnumbered, Walker retreated from the scene, but the fight resumed when he returned with eight or nine fellow soldiers. Reinforcement for the workers soon arrived from nearby rope-walks and the soldiers were beaten back to the barracks once again. But about forty of them returned a short time later with clubs and knives, and a full-scale rumble ensued. The following days were filled with rumors among citizens of military plots against the city and within the military of individual soldiers abducted by citizens.

In a confrontation three days later, a boy was hit in the face by the barrel of a musket. Soon there was yelling in the street, and church bells began tolling. Men began shouting "Fire!" and people poured out of their houses and into the streets. Private Hugh White, who had hit the boy, was alone and cornered by the crowd against the steps of the Custom House. Frightened, he loaded his musket and fixed the bayonet. The crowd shouted insults, dared him to fire, and pelted him with snowballs.

The fire alarms caused commotion throughout the city, and crowds began gathering at Murphy's Barracks and the Dock Square. A soldier had run out of the barracks and aimed his musket at a crowd forming in the street, but he was knocked over by his officers before he could fire it and was forced back inside. Another group of redcoats, unarmed but for a shovel, met a hail of snowballs and was forced to the barracks. As crowds throughout town converged at the Custom House, Captain Thomas Preston sensed that Private White, still alone and surrounded, was in danger. He hesitated, knowing that any show of force would further rile the mob, then sent seven of his men through the crowd to save White.

Church bells continued to toll and more people poured into the street. Insults and snowballs flying toward them, the small column of grenadiers made their way through the crowd and loaded their weapons. Reaching the Custom House, the beleaguered Private White joined their ranks. On the way back across King Street volleys from the crowd intensified. Rioters dared them to fire their weapons. "You can't kill us all," someone shouted. A justice of the peace showed up to read the Riot Act to the crowd but was pelted with snowballs and sent scurrying down the street.

Closing in against the row of bayonets, men began shoving each other toward the soldiers, those behind jumping up on the backs of those in front. A wooden club knocked one of the redcoats to the ground, his musket falling by his side. Swearing and struggling to his feet, he retrieved the gun and fired it into the crowd. Fists flew, sticks clashed against bayonets, more shots rang out, and five citizens lay dead in the street.

This was a horrible tragedy for the dead and wounded and for their families, but it was exactly what the growing revolutionary movement needed. Here were heroes, men who died for the cause and for what they believed in. Colonial Americans were already beginning to say that having but one life, it would be best given to the country. Now there were real people who had given their lives.

Mounting the wave of public opinion, the Sons of Liberty staged dramatic funeral processions for the fallen heroes, and news of the "massacre" spread far and wide through the colonies and across the Atlantic. Paul Revere printed and sold thousands of copies of a grossly propagandistic rendition of the event, showing redcoats lined in formation, firing on a helpless crowd of peace-loving citizens at the cold-blooded command of Captain Preston. This event and the spin given it by the radicals would divide the public into "us" and "them."

Mob violence was an extremely important element of the revolutionary movement, but to be effective, it had to be carefully crafted and controlled. At the public awareness stage of the movement, the most useful and creative violence was that *aimed at themselves*. With British troops present at a mob scene, the purpose of violence was not to achieve tactical advantage but to provoke response. Until public opinion was securely aimed toward independence, the hearts and minds of Colonial Americans were the real targets of the revolutionary movement, not the redcoats.

Redcoats were mere symbols. Had British troops been mobbed and killed by unruly citizens (an equally likely scenario), the outcome would have been disastrous for the cause of independence.

When troops were not present, the mob was useful for the tactic of intimidation. It was used throughout the revolutionary period to enforce the boycott on British goods. "Importers" sometimes found themselves threatened and their property destroyed by crowds of self-righteous "patriots," but more often than not, this was unnecessary. It was enough for most merchants to know that the mob was alive and well and that some of their own people were at its command.

By December 1773, Sam Adams and his followers got the chance to use the mob for both tactical advantage and provocation. Three British vessels had sailed into Boston Harbor loaded with tea. Due to the earlier disturbances in Boston, Parliament had repealed taxes on almost everything but remained determined to tax tea. The revolutionaries were equally determined to resist the tax and did not want to allow a precedent by allowing its payment by these three ships. The ships remained at the wharf for three weeks as negotiations proceeded to de-fuse the crisis. The town wanted the ships sent back to England and the Crown wanted them unloaded and the tax paid. Adams kept the mob carefully within bounds as the situation intensified. Then, at a public meeting, all else having failed, he gave a prearranged secret signal for the mob to attack. About one hundred men dressed as Mohawk Indians boarded the ships and threw the cargo overboard into Boston Harbor. This was the signal act of the American Revolution.

This little piece of street theater was as unambiguously illegal as it could possibly be. It was designed to be *provocatively* illegal. Illegality is not always revolutionary, but revolution is always illegal. A revolution has to demonstrate the existing regime's inability to enforce its own laws. It has to violate the law in an especially public manner, and it has to get away with it. Adams and his followers knew that there would be serious consequences, and that is precisely what they wanted to see.

Parliament responded directly to the Boston Tea Party by sending more troops to Boston in an attempt to enforce the law. The harbor was closed to commercial traffic until the destroyed goods were paid for. As a result of the British escalation, resistance to British rule increased in all the colonies, and weapons were gathered and hidden in rural areas just outside port cities, including Boston. This led to the British military sending patrols into the countryside and the confrontation at Lexington Green.

Sam Adams and the Sons of Liberty did it all. By seizing the raw material of inner-city violence and forging it into a political weapon, they created a new nation. They understood more than anyone else that debating societies and boycott associations are fine but that to create a new sense of *being*, you need violence or something like it. Colonial Americans would not begin thinking of themselves as Americans for the sake of taxes — they needed to feel a threat to their lives. Intellectual arguments would produce intellectual solutions; economic tactics would produce economic measures; only physical threats to life and property would produce changes in how people understood who they actually *were*. We can almost see the crowds surrounding Preston's men at the Custom House shouting to the Redcoats: "Fire away! We dare you! Please do it! Only you can make us into Americans!"

Were the Sons of Liberty the terrorists of the American Revolution? Is intimidation a lesser former of terrorism? There is no doubt that Sam Adams and his followers used fear of bodily harm to change political consciousness, which is the same prime motivator of human behavior favored by modern terrorist groups. British Loyalists in Colonial America felt the same fear we feel now when bombs go off in Ulster, Baghdad, or Jerusalem. A customs official in Colonial Boston, watching a mob forming outside his front door, understood its political message on the same level of consciousness as we now understand the political message of Sinn Fein, Hamas, or Al Qaeda. This is what made the American Revolution revolutionary. Violence is the wedge of human identity: British citizens in the colonies converted to Americanism only when violence forced them to choose one side or the other. They became new people as they reached for weapons and began to shoot and be shot by their former selves. Political identity is not limited to the plane of social and economic interaction. It reaches down into the human body: We are what the cells of our bodies have us think we are. Only danger can change it.

Americans owe their identity as Americans to the seeds of violence sewn by the Sons of Liberty. But for the most part the Sons did not harm those not directly involved in the issues they protested. They did not bomb public buildings and destroy innocent life. They did not hesitate to use force and their tactics were often destructive, but their targets were almost always inanimate. They preferred the threat of violence to the real thing. They used the grim and dirty realities of fear and hatred to their advantage, but they did so in a controlled and measured way. Not altogether innocent of what we now call political terror, they did not cross certain lines of basic human decency. They used force without overusing it, creating the divisiveness of the revolutionary movement without alienating public opinion from their own side. A sizable and decisive portion of the American population converted to the identity the Sons of Liberty created and went on to win the struggle they defined.

The revolutionary movement to create a united human identity is destined to meet violence in the course of its struggle. But unlike the Sons of Liberty, it need not provoke it. Globalists, like the Americans, are confronted with the daunting and dangerous task of transforming human identity, but unlike revolutionary Americans, they need not create sides to define the conflict. They must instead demonstrate that sides to the struggle do not exist. The transformation they bring about will be from many to one, not one to another. The wedge of violence and hatred will be used against them, but they will have no way to use it themselves. There is no one who is not who they are. Those who oppose them may consider themselves enemies, but the true identity of humanity, once achieved, can have no human enemy.

Terror will, inevitably, play a role in the transformation from national to global consciousness as it did in the transformation from British to American consciousness. It is already built into the weapons we have made; in time we will see it with our eyes and feel it in our bellies. There will be a passage through the state of nature. The less we understand of what we are doing, the more actual terror we will experience. The more we understand the meaning of tools that can destroy all people, the more we may experience their terror in potential form. With foresight, we may avoid actual terror altogether. Either way, we will die to what we now are before becoming what we will be.

The crisis will come in the course of time: We will all feel the hollowness in our stomachs felt by the mob in Boston as the muskets thundered on King Street. There will be a moment of death in the air. Will we be prepared for that moment? Will there be direction — any idea of what is happening and where we are going? Will there be a sense of who we are transforming ourselves into? Or will there be violence and confusion without the chance for order and creation?

Nationality will one day die at the hand of its own violence to humanity. This we may know. We cannot know that humanity will emerge in its place.

25. May 1971

STANDING ON THE CORNER, HOLDING A SIGN, ONE CANNOT help but feel a little foolish. Most people don't care. Nine out of ten drive by, trying not to look. Their faces are blank, intent on work, television shows, and shopping. What were they thinking a minute ago, before they rounded the corner? How did we suddenly appear, standing where they always drive, presenting them with the question of war? Is this the place for such a question? A few passersby thank us, smile, wave, even cheer. One asks for our Web site. Others call us traitors, fighters for Saddam, as bad as the terrorists. One shouts out his window that we disgust him, another that we should be shot for our disloyalty. I am continually amazed by the violent response to peace.

But most of them just drive by, looking past us, as if we were beggars on the street. And we are. We are asking them for something, pleading, pulling on their minds. How can we get them out of their everyday mindset? How can we get them to think they need something we have to offer? This is what it feels like to be a door-to-door salesman or a telemarketer. Demonstrating in public is embarrassing and of questionable value. Is this the way to save the world from nuclear annihilation? Isn't there some better way to make people think?

I saw a documentary the other night on Watergate. It began in summer 1972 when President Nixon was well on his way to being elected to a second term. He illegally bugged the headquarters of the Democratic Party at the Watergate Hotel because the Democrats were running an antiwar candidate. As I remember it, Nixon was way ahead in the polls and not even campaigning. He didn't have to. Nobody liked the war anymore, but they trusted him with it more than with McGovern. He was going to beat McGovern no matter what. And he did, by a landslide: forty-nine states to one.

But that was not enough for Nixon. He wanted absolute control. He did not like opposition. People who spoke against his policies were disloyal to the country, and people who disagreed with him were traitors. I did not realize how uptight and power-hungry he was. He thought of himself as embodying America — and he did, in a way. Most Americans looked at Nixon as someone who could pull the country through a rough time. They knew he was trying to end the war and that he would not give in to the Communists in Vietnam or anywhere else. A lot of Americans did not like Nixon and did not think he was right in any moral sense, but they also saw him as someone who could get them out of a bad situation. So why did he bug the Watergate? He had the public behind him; why did he risk it all on a two-bit gangster operation — complete with burglars, bribes, threats, and money laundering — when it was so obviously unnecessary? Why did he lie and cheat and subvert the very system he claimed to love? Why did he make lists of enemies and use federal agencies to harass them? Why was he so afraid of little people like me?

It was not enough for Richard Nixon to win elections. He wanted to be right. He wanted the country to follow him, to look up to him, to admire him. The country, as it turned out, did not admire him but was using him to get out of something they knew was wrong. He did not want to be used; he wanted to be loved.

For most Americans, the war was over by 1972. The fighting continued and people kept getting killed, but the war, for most, was over. We were defending a regime that was not defending itself: a regime that did not even like itself, and American boys — sons and husbands and young fathers — were being killed every

day. We were killing Vietcong and they were killing us, and it
made no sense. There was nothing in it for anybody, but it went
on because it had not yet stopped. Americans wanted Nixon to
stop the war; he still wanted to win it in some glorious, honorable
way.

What made the documentary interesting for me was that
Nixon was so concerned about the demonstrations against the war.
I hadn't known that. I thought he didn't notice and didn't care. But
apparently he did. There was a lot of footage shown from a
demonstration in May of 1971 that apparently drove Nixon up a
wall. He made a big deal of appearing unaffected, pretending to
be working on other "presidential" things, but he was extremely
upset and uptight. He watched it continuously on television and
made sure that one of his henchmen updated him every half hour
on where the crowd was, what the speakers were saying, and
how many arrests there were. He also, interestingly, had to keep
an eye on the defense of the capital. In addition to the D.C. police
force, the national guard had to be called out to keep the streets
open and the government running. He needed the presence of
an armed force — thousands of soldiers — to show that he was
still in charge and still president, and everybody was watching
him trying to do it. It didn't look much like a popular democracy.
Everyone was seeing how much trouble he was having just to
keep the war going, and a lot of people were going to be thinking
about what the demonstrators were saying. A lot of people might
think the demonstrators were right instead of him.

And they were right. Not because of anything they said or did
but because the war they were against was so plainly wrong.
People were suffering and fighting and dying for nothing. The
demonstrators didn't make the war wrong: All they did was show
it to the public. The war was going to be wrong or not on its own
merits. And the demonstrators didn't end the war either — the
public did, after they saw what the war was. It was the public,
Nixon's own "silent majority," who decided that the war was

wrong and wanted it over. They just needed Nixon to clean up the dirty work. This drove Nixon mad. But the public would not have ended the war without the demonstrators. They needed the war stuck in their faces.

I did not realize this at the time. I knew the demonstrations had some effect, but I had no idea how much. The body bags and the death count did more than the vigils and protests, but every war has body bags and death counts; not every war has vigils and protests. I think that the demonstrations brought to the conscience of America the horror of war in general and the injustice of this war in particular. I also think that the demonstrations brought down a very corrupt presidential administration that could have ruined the American system. Bringing down the Nixon administration was not the intent of the demonstrations, but the president's stance against the moral clarity they presented to the public brought him down. He could not tolerate someone else appearing right to his public.

I did not realize how effective the demonstration of May 1971 was, even though, interestingly, I was there. I was not a leader or an organizer — just a foot soldier following the plan as I understood it. I had been to a few demonstrations before, but I was no big campus radical and did not belong to SDS or the Weather Underground or anything else, for that matter. I just wanted the war over. But it was getting frustrating. It seemed, by that point, that no matter how many demonstrations we had, nothing was working. So I decided to up my commitment a notch or two. People had gone to considerable extremes in the name of war, I reasoned to myself, so why shouldn't I go just a little farther in the name of peace?

We came from out of town in the back of a rented U-Haul truck, about thirty of us. There was a whole weekend of the usual demonstrations: a march on the White House, a rally at the Monument, etc. — I do not remember the particulars of the first day or two. The real demonstration we had come for — the one that was shown on the documentary about Watergate — was Monday morning. Most of the demonstrators had gone home. There were only about 15,000 of us left, and we were going to shut down the city of Washington. No more business as usual. If they weren't going to shut the war down, we were going to shut them down.

We went through some rudimentary training in nonviolent tactics. We practiced sitting down, locking arms, going limp, etc., and we even practiced being polite to the police. We learned to say "Yes, sir," and "No, sir," and not to call them "pigs." Some role-played the police, swinging newspaper billy clubs over our heads and threatening arrest. It all seemed pretty simple: We would walk out onto major bridges and intersections and just sit down and wait to be arrested, blocking traffic for as long as we could.

We were camped at Potomac Park, south of the Mall. There were police on all sides of us, but they stayed out of our encampment for the most part. I remember people throwing rocks at one armored police vehicle attempting to drive through the area on patrol. Several people jumped on it and tried to smash its windows, but somehow it threw them off and sped away. I remember thinking that the police were afraid of us — at least here on our turf. Helicopters flew over us in a constant stream. There were eight or ten or more of them, one after another, circling overhead without pause. Most of them were police and national guard; some of them were media. They were so loud we could barely hear a thing. Wherever people tried to meet in groups, the helicopters would fly even lower. It was impossible to plan, to organize, to think. People were wandering around, wondering what to do, and there was a lot of anger and confusion. Finally, we heard that the police were kicking us out of the park. I thought there would be mass rioting and violence, but there wasn't any that I saw. We reminded ourselves that our fight was not with the police, so we picked up and left. But I felt cheated because many who would have demonstrated the next day had nowhere to stay and left town. Our group stayed at a house in Maryland. Our assignment was to block the Roosevelt Bridge. We were to approach from the D.C. side, walk up onto the bridge, and sit down. Another group would do the same on the Arlington side. About four o'clock in the morning, we sent out a scout to have a look at the bridge. He came back an hour later and said there were national guardsmen standing shoulder-to-shoulder along the entire length of the bridge, on both sides. They had guns and bayonets. Both approaches to the bridge were swarming with police in riot gear. We heard on the news that the police and national guardsmen in the whole city totaled around 16,000, slightly more, we later learned, than there were of us. We climbed into the back of the U-Haul.

The ride was bumpy and dark. I was afraid, but I needed to be doing this. This was where I stood. I felt like a paratrooper about to jump out of an airplane. I thought of all the millions of brave men who had gone off to war not knowing what was going to happen to them. This was not that bad. We knew they wouldn't try to kill us, but that's all we knew. We were in the dark, quite literally. We had no idea what would happen in the next few minutes, but we knew something would happen.

We heard shouting and screaming outside the truck and some of the vilest language imaginable. I thought we were hearing fellow demonstrators already on the scene, young people capable of any level of obscenity. But it turned out to be the police, swearing at us. The truck swerved suddenly and came to an abrupt stop, throwing us about violently in the dark. The shouting and cursing grew louder. We sat there, in the dark, wondering what was happening outside.

Suddenly, the back door of the truck flew open and blinding daylight rushed in. We all struggled to our feet, shielding our eyes. When I turned to look out the back, all I could see were police, screaming, swinging batons, cursing, and hitting people's legs and backs as they jumped off the truck. I was hit only slightly as I struggled to get out the back and down to the street through the swarm of police.

People were running in every direction. A lot of people were hit, there was some blood, but nobody was seriously injured. I noticed that the hood of the truck was up and that the police had cut the distributor wires. I ran to where I saw some of our people trying to gather, but the police were soon running after us. I stopped on a side street to help a woman who had been hit in the shin with a baton. I was designated a medic and had a small first-aid kit with me. As I opened the bag to treat her wound, a policeman came around the corner swinging his club. I shouted at him that I was trying to deal with an injury, but he kept coming at me. As I started to run he yelled at me to stop, but I kept going. He gave up the chase after about a block and a half.

Several blocks away I met up with four or five others, and we decided to cut our losses and just get out of there. We were completely outmaneuvered, the whole group was scattered, and we had no chance of getting to the bridge. We never even saw it. We were not there to play games with the police, and there was nothing further to be done. We walked all the way back. We never even got a chance to be nonviolent. They had won.

According to the documentary, more than half the demonstrators, around eight thousand, were arrested that day, more than in any other day in American history. We felt utterly beaten, and the war went on. We had no idea.

26. Satyagraha

From the beginning I had strongly disliked the necessity of
dispersing these non-violent crowds, and although the injuries
inflicted on the lawbreakers were almost invariably very slight
the idea of using force against such men was very different
from the more cogent need for using it against violent rioters
who were endangering other men's lives. At the same time I
realized that the law-breakers could not be allowed to continue their deliberate misbehavior without any action by the
police. As time went on I found to my dismay that my intense
dislike of the whole procedure grew to such an extent that on
every occasion when the Congress staged a large demonstration I felt a severe physical nausea which prevented me from
taking food until the crisis was over. I knew on each occasion
that the crisis would be over in a matter of hours and that the
crowd would disperse or be dispersed and the leaders would
call off the demonstration. I was at a loss to understand why I
should be physically affected by it. I remembered that I had
had no such feelings on occasions of serious rioting in
Bombay or in my earlier pursuits of frontier raiders. I thought
then, and I still think, that I was largely influenced by the
feeling that whatever we did the result was to the advantage of
the Congress policy and that the policy of our Government in
dealing with it was wrong.

— *John Court Curry, English police officer, Bombay, 1930,
during one of Gandhi's campaigns*[25]

WE CANNOT NOW TELL WHAT THE MOVEMENT IS FOR. There is no way to know. It will become clear only when it is past and the truth is revealed. What the end will be cannot be said, because there is no end: There are only means. The truth can be urged by acting truthfully, but it is never a possession. Truth claimed as property is backed up behind what is thought and diverted from its natural course. It must be allowed to flow through those who act and through those who oppose. We stand not for ideas, but for the power of truth we are trying to know: satyagraha.

In South Africa, Mohandas Gandhi stood for the racial equality of whites and Indians but not of "kaffirs." He wanted his people to be treated equally with Europeans. Black people were not part of the movement. Later, in India, he stood for independence from British rule but also for rejection of the modern world and a return to preindustrial Indian village society. For India to be free, he thought, the spinning wheel would have to replace the factory. But he did not impede the flow of truth with these ideas, and the world learned from him much more than he knew how to teach.

In India, it was illegal to possess salt not obtained from the British salt monopoly. The people of India did not have a right to their own resources without paying a tax to the British imperial government. In the spring of 1930, Gandhi left the town of Sabarmati with seventy-eight followers and marched two hundred miles to the sea just south of Ahmadabad, stopping many times along the way. The world press followed him at every step.

When he arrived at the beach, he picked up a handful of salt off the sand and thereby committed a punishable crime. He was arrested. Soon Indians throughout the country were following his example, making salt anywhere and everywhere in open defiance of the law. More than sixty thousand were arrested. Before going to jail Gandhi wrote a letter to the British viceroy stating his intention to confront the British monopoly at the Dharasana Salt Works. Twenty-five hundred marchers showed up at the plant. A select group advanced and was ordered to retreat. What ensued was witnessed and reported to the world by Webb Miller, a correspondent for United Press:

> Suddenly, at a word of command, scores of native policemen rushed upon the advancing marchers and rained blows on their heads with their steel-shod lathis. Not one of the marchers even raised an arm to fend off the blows. They went down like nine-pins.... The waiting crowd of marchers groaned and sucked in their breath in sympathetic pain at every blow. Those struck down fell sprawling, unconscious or writhing with fractured skulls or broken shoulders.... The survivors, without breaking ranks, silently and doggedly marched on until struck down.

After the first column was beaten down, another advanced in its place, and then a third. More than three hundred people were injured and two died.[26] The world saw the truth of British rule in India.

Satyagraha has to be true, illegal, and public. It has to say something that people recognize in their individual conscience, do something that forces them to confront conscience, and do it in a way that externalizes conscience. It must reach down to the part of us that is potentially violent and find peace in that place. If there is no peace there, it must make peace before it may move on, because it seeks this same place of peace in others. It must find it in order to show where it is. In confronting injustice, it must avoid violence but also replace violence. It must do what violence normally does. It does this by risking provocation of violence in the opposition. It externalizes conscience by forcing the opposition to see the place of its own potential violence and helping it find peace in that place.

In 1963, Birmingham, Alabama, was the "biggest, toughest, most segregated city in the South." Martin Luther King Jr. knew that a victory there would externalize the conscience of the entire nation. He was not from Birmingham and was resented by both blacks and whites as an outsider. The black Baptist clergy voted overwhelmingly to oppose the campaign, and of four hundred black Baptist churches, only fourteen opened their doors to him for mass meetings.[27] But he brought satyagraha to Birmingham.

Desegregation of public facilities in the downtown shopping district was the objective. There would be sit-ins and peaceful marches and demonstrations. But police chief Bull Connor refused to issue permits for peaceful marches and demonstrations, and marchers soon found themselves arrested for "parading without a permit." The marches went on, and the arrests continued. The city issued an injunction against further demonstrations, but King announced to reporters that he would not obey it because it violated the fundamental constitutional rights of speech and assembly. He was arrested and jailed the next day.

But the word was out. People all over the country were watching Truth marching through the streets of Birmingham. King was kept in solitary confinement without a mattress or a pillow to lie on until President Kennedy made a phone call to Birmingham. A few days later, as he was released, six thousand elementary and high school children marched to city hall. They were blocked by police and then attacked with police dogs and high-pressure fire hoses as the cameras rolled. There were injuries and arrests.

Children kept marching the next day and the day after that, as the jails filled and the nation watched in horror. More than three thousand people were arrested. "As hard as it is, we must meet physical force with soul force," King told his followers. "We're struggling not to save ourselves alone, but we're struggling to save the soul of this nation."[28]

Pressure mounted from within the city and from across the nation. Business leaders and companies with branches in Birmingham called for desegregation and compromise. The immediate result was the Birmingham Truce Agreement, which called for desegregation of lunch counters, fitting rooms, restrooms, and drinking fountains — but the real result was an enlargement of what it means to be American. The conscience of the nation had been struck.

Martin Luther King Jr. created a bigger America — one that more people could live in. He did it by enforcing the constitutional rights of black people in America, but the effect — the true change — was in white people. It was white people who made more room in their minds. Black people already knew the full truth of segregation. King did it by showing white people, on television, what the truth of segregation was — what they would have to do to keep it. Truth flowed through him and his ideas and through the bravery of his followers, but it flowed as much through the politicians and police who opposed him. It was the politicians and the police who convinced the white public. Here was white America, for all the world to see, excluding black people from the circle of full humanity. This was the truth of segregation. Martin Luther King showed white people what they looked like, and they did not like it. So they changed.

In a far more brutally racist society, Nelson Mandela spent twenty-seven years in South African prisons for leading a movement against apartheid. He believed in racial equality — a simple truth. In 1962, he told a judge who sentenced him to prison: "If I had my time over I would do the same again. So would any man who dares call himself a man."

Blacks made up seventy percent of the South African population but were restricted to thirteen percent of the land. They were not allowed to live or work outside of their "homelands" without a pass proving that they worked for a European. Many did work for Europeans as servants or in the mines but could not get passes for their wives and children. This forced families to be separated for long periods.

Any black person caught outside his homeland without a pass was subject to arrest. He was, therefore, a potential criminal merely for being what he was. In 1960, the Pan Africanist Congress, a splinter group from Mandela's African National

Congress, organized a protest in Sharpeville against the hated pass law. As the demonstrators assembled peacefully, police arrived on the scene and fired into the crowd. Sixty-nine were killed and one hundred and eighty wounded.[29]

Mandela did not see his wife or children for years at a time. He missed family birthdays, anniversaries, weddings, graduations, and funerals. He spent most of his time, year after year, sitting in a solitary cell, forbidden to speak, sing, or pray out loud. In summer he was taken to a quarry to cut limestone. He developed back trouble, high blood pressure, and damaged eyesight. He was allowed to write to his wife every six months. She was allowed to visit him for thirty minutes about every two years, through a small window, speaking by telephone in front of prison authorities. At 2:00 a.m. on May 12, 1969, she was arrested as her children slept. No charges were announced. Her children did not know what happened to her for a year and a half.

In 1973 Mandela was offered his freedom if he would settle in his homeland, a move that would encourage other blacks to accept the apartheid policy of "separate development." Mandela refused and remained in prison for another seventeen years.

In Soweto in 1976, between six hundred and one thousand blacks were killed by police. Most of them were children. The world took notice. Throughout the 1970s and early 1980s, television crews sent pictures around the world of black people throwing rocks and white police officers answering with bullets. Though he remained isolated behind bars and invisible to the media, Mandela became a symbol of black South Africa itself — imprisoned. Protest movements, economic sanctions, and boycotts were organized around the world.

When he was finally released in 1990, Mandela told his followers, "Take your guns, your knives, and your *pangas* [machetes] and throw them into the sea." Blacks should not be struggling against whites or against other blacks, but against apartheid. "Unlike white people anywhere else in Africa," he said, "whites in

South Africa belong here — this is their home. We want them to live here with us and to share power with us." He bore no ill will to those who had kept him from his family for so many years. Smiling and waving to the cameras, he walked away from the prison gates and set about establishing a just society that included all South Africans. On May 2, 1994, he was elected president of South Africa.

Violence was called for in India, America, and South Africa. Violence did, in fact, surround the movements led by Gandhi, King, and Mandela. But nonviolence won the day. Nonviolence was successful not because it kept people from being hurt (which it did not) but because it took the place of violence and did a better job of changing human consciousness than violence would have done. It accomplished what violence normally accomplishes but went further by expanding the scope of human consciousness.

In India, violence would have led to independence at the expense of a long and bloody war of liberation. India would not be the world leader in peaceful social change. In South Africa, violence would have ended apartheid but with the expense of endless civil war. That country would not be a leader on the African continent nor in nonviolent resistance movements around the world. In America, violence might have achieved equality for blacks and whites, but it would not have expanded what America is. It would not have made us what we have become. Whites would have granted equality to blacks through the necessity that only fear can provide.

But *nonviolence* is not a good word for what Gandhi, King, and Mandela did. It describes not what they did but what they did not do. *Nonviolence* means anything other than violence; it can mean avoiding danger by standing on the sidelines or staying home when the going gets rough. It can mean doing nothing at all.

Satyagraha, on the other hand, means the use of force — *truth force*. It means action. Satyagraha is inherently nonviolent, but it is also inherently proactive. It seeks targets that stimulate the conscience of the opposition, thereby revealing truth in the course of confrontation. Opposition to the movement becomes as important as the movement itself. Neither side in a confrontation is altogether right, and neither side can say what truth will emerge. But the right questions and the right points of confrontation provoke answers that are later seen to be true. Therefore, the goal of satyagraha is to find the right questions and the right way to ask them. It is not concerned with answers.

This is as it should be, for answers close the question and remove meaning from social evolution. Racial equality seems obvious to most people now because it has become an answer. But its meaning cannot be appreciated without knowing the enormity of its existence as a question.

The meaning of King's or Mandela's or Gandhi's lives can be understood only in terms of the question before it was answered. We know now that they were right to confront unjust authority, but we know it only because they did it and succeeded. People did not know it at the time. Most people were too afraid to ask the question. With shootings, bombings, and daily threats to themselves and their families, it is a wonder that anyone was brave enough to ask what they asked. Satyagraha is the pursuit of truth before it is revealed.

Let us then advocate global unity but not claim it as truth. Let us rather ask the questions that will provoke the truth: What will we do when the climate changes? How will we live when there are too many people? How will we address economic globalization; loss of cultural and ecological diversity; and poverty, terrorism, hunger, and infectious disease when they arrive at our doorstep? How will we get to work when the oil runs out? What will we eat when the soil has eroded? Who will we turn to when nations resort to nuclear war? Properly asked, truth will come from these questions, but how may they be asked? Must the questions become desperate before they are answered? Must we wait until they break down the door? How may satyagraha break down the door before it is too late?

Now, at the beginning of the twenty-first century, there are many streams running together: resource depletion, overpopulation, environmental disaster, climate change, weapons of mass destruction. Is this coincidence? Is it chance that four or five cataclysmic crises converge now — in our lifetime? Can they be handled separately? Can any one of them be handled at all in a divided world? What is their connection, and how can the truth of their connection be revealed? Can the questions that need answers be asked in a divided world?

That is the problem. There is no world of which these questions may be asked. We have only a vague concept of who we are on Earth, and no means of acting as humans. There is no *we* that can *do*. With no means of acting, the questions provoke only helplessness and despair. Where King, Gandhi, and Mandela discovered and confronted clear symbols of racism and injustice, there is no clear symbol of the world divided against itself: It is everywhere and nowhere in particular. When we protest against war, it is aimed at the policy of a particular government, and not against the underlying divisions that cause war. When we protest against industrial pollution or commercial globalization, it is aimed at the behavior of particular institutions and corporations and not at the absence of unified commercial, labor, and environmental regulation. It is difficult to protest against a division or against an absence — the protest itself falls into the division and into the absence. We are asking the right questions but in ways that do not create new consciousness.

The challenge of satyagraha is to ask the same questions in a manner that stimulates thinking toward the creation of global political tools that will make solutions possible. We have the job to do, but first we have to make the tools to do it. With a perceived means of solution, the same world problems provoke thought and creativity instead of guilt and despair. A new sense of being arises in response to questions well asked, and a new sense of self emerges that welcomes challenges that make life interesting and meaningful.

Can humans create new ways of organizing themselves? Can we do things we have not thought of before? Can love, hope, and compassion, implicit in the ideal of human unity, have a practical as well as a spiritual place in human affairs? Can they solve the problems of war, pollution, and economic justice, or if not, can they create the means by which they may be solved?

The movement for human unity can have no enemies. Many will oppose it, but it will have no enemies of its own. It will be purely positive. But it will organize against specific targets, first among them war. Not this war or that war, but war itself. Not against people who promote or fight one side or another of a war, but against the structure of sovereign relations that makes war necessary.

Being against war is a double negative: It is against that which is against people. But it is not necessarily positive. It becomes positive only when expressed as compassion for all people, including those who make war. Until then it remains one negative on top of another. As compassion, being against war stimulates the externalization of conscience. Organized public opposition to the violence and injustice of war, expressed with compassion, becomes satyagraha.

Opposition to war in the twenty-first century does not mean opposition to all wars in all times — it means opposition to war in our time. It does not assume that war is never justified. We need not unfight wars of the past — we need only *not* fight them in the future.

Fighting and dying for country is the ultimate altruism of the age of nations, and we should appreciate the bravery of people who have won and sustained a unique civilization for us and for our children. But theirs was an age when wars could be fought and won; ours is not. Theirs was a time when officially sanctioned violence could preserve hearth and home; ours is not. Theirs was an era in which warfare could be construed as more pragmatic than the continuing search for peace; ours is not. War in our own time is not "realistic" or "hardheaded" in any sense.

Satyagraha, because it is truth, will show the truth of war then and the truth of war now. We need only allow it to flow. It will show that war is not the problem of a particular people or a particular government but of all people everywhere — and that it can be addressed only from a global perspective. The truth of common humanity will reveal itself through well-directed questions that confront what we have always thought. It will move through those who believe in it and through those who oppose it.

When we do not have to fight each other we will see the world more clearly. We will feel more secure and confident in our presence on Earth and, in that security and confidence, care for the forests and the atmosphere, tend the oceans and the croplands, and secure the political and economic justice that people want. With a sense of self that does not depend on human enemies, humanity will be poised to act on its own behalf and on behalf of a living planet that depends on human compassion.

I do not know what tactics and strategies will be adopted, but I do know that the movement for global unity will begin in the streets. It will not happen in legislatures and seminars and closed meetings. It will not happen in books and magazines and Web sites. All of these will be necessary, but they will not change who we think we are. They will not change all of us, together.

King, Mandela, Gandhi, and Adams knew that the changes they sought would be changes in collective being — not mere changes in fashion and opinion — and that this depth of change must happen in the streets, with people looking on. They created situations in which the opposition would demonstrate power relations for them to the public. They challenged existing power relations and risked the potential violence enfolded within them. They wrote and spoke in closed meetings to refine the message and to inspire a following, but the message was then taken outside to those who would *not* follow. It was taken to those who did not agree and to the far greater numbers of those who did not care. These are people found in public places. Satyagraha challenges injustice and oppression, but mostly it challenges apathy.

The movement for world unity will be built on what has been taught and learned through satyagraha. When you call a meeting in a building, there is a framework, both physical and psychic, around what is discussed. People who are interested in the topic will attend. There will have to be meetings in buildings, and you will need to call them, but the doing itself must be done outside in public. People who have no interest in the topic must be exposed to it. They must see what you are doing whether or not they want to look. They should be confronted gently, politely, and nonviolently. *They* are the people who need to be asked the question. Some will support you, others will oppose; most will pass you by. Some will shower you with praise, others with contempt; most will shrug you off. But in time, if you stay there, they will see you. They will ask the questions you ask. That is all you can do.

The meaning is in the process, not the result. There is no end.

Part VI — The Final

27. The World Budget

IN 2003, WE SPENT ABOUT A TRILLION DOLLARS FOR WEAPONS and military training. That's one million million dollars: about $100 million every hour of every day. If we preferred, we could take $78 billion, or about eight percent of this amount, and use it to prevent worldwide soil erosion, eliminate starvation and malnutrition, provide reproductive health for every woman on Earth, provide safe drinking water for everyone, prevent acid rain, and eliminate illiteracy.[30] But we do not prefer. We want the guns.

Only people can spend money. We spend it according to what is important to us. We spend more money on ways to kill people because we fear people more than anything else. We fear other people more than hunger, poverty, disease, pollution, resource depletion, climate change, economic injustice, or ecological disaster. We fear them more than we fear war. Interestingly, we fear people more than we fear nuclear holocaust. If we did not, we would spend our money differently.

But there is no *we* deciding these things. There is no world budget. There is no council or legislature or assembly of representatives appropriating half the resources of human civilization for injuring, capturing, shooting, and dismembering human beings. If there were, I suspect it would be voted out of office. There are instead many separate *we*'s spending money this way, and we keep them in office because, for the most part, they do what we want them to do. The greatest democracies on Earth choose guns and tanks and nuclear bombs over schools and hospitals because their greatest fear is of other people. Does this make sense?

The primary purpose of human civilization has always been the organization of potential violence for reasons of security. Security is number one. The shell of security protecting commerce, industry, and the arts is an armed suppression of violence from within and from without: a threat of violence to the violent. This is how security is secured. After security, a civilization can think about schools and hospitals and taking care of its people in a civilized manner. On average, a civil society spends about half its resources on security. It is not surprising, then, that of the approximately $2 trillion dollars that governments tax and spend these days, about $1 trillion goes for military purposes.

I think this is as it should be. The primary purpose of civilization should be the organization or reorganization of potential violence into armies and police forces. Security should be first, and it is worth half our public resources. I am willing to contribute my share because I do not wish to be mugged in the street or to lose my home and family to an invading force. I am willing to pay what it costs.

But if we can get security for less than $1 trillion a year, we should consider the option, and I think we have that option right now. At this particular moment in history, we have the opportunity to buy greater security at a bargain price. But it is available only if we act now. We can get it much cheaper than it is worth and save hundreds of billions for other things.

The wonder of global unity is that the cost of basic security will be a fraction of what it is now. An armed force will be necessary to maintain order, but it will be much smaller than the forces we have now. There will be only one force and no competition among forces to be strongest and deadliest and no race for armed supremacy. There will be a single shell of security covering everyone and no threat from the outside. Military expenditures will drop to a tiny portion of what they are now, and there will be larger budget allocations for everything else. We will have to find other ways to spend the money.

Global unity would be worth the price if military expenditures remained $1 trillion a year — but they won't.

28. The Dynamic of Enclosure

AND WHAT WILL CHANGE WHEN THE CAPACITY TO KILL people is no longer the organizing principle of civilization? What will change when there are no people we may dismiss as foreigners? Who will we be to each other when there is no enemy and the sphere of human concern encloses the earth? Will we know who we are when there is no one we are not?

When it is done it will be as nothing. We will rise, work, rest, mourn, and celebrate much as we do now. Life will be as before. Peace will be the air itself: breathed by all, noticed by none: the absence of what no longer exists. Our children will not know what it is. There will be less to stir the blood, less talk of blood, less blood, less hatred of blood, less passion. Culture will no longer be in the blood. Our children will live because we did not do what our fathers did, doing instead what had never been done — what our fathers could not do. Our children will not know that we wondered what to do and did not know. They will think what we did became real because it happened, not knowing that we superimposed reality with wishful images and made them real. Reality was going the other way. The images will be what they live, but for them it will be something that happened long ago. They will not see flowers fall from guns, bombers become butterflies, long armies turning back. They will not hear the gentle dove roar. They will not feel the flow of love over mountains and down valleys, across oceans, thinning, and swelling back to itself. Only we will see these things and know what did not happen. So much did not happen. They will not feel the moment of loss we all felt at one time together. The crisis will have passed. They will not see for themselves the triumph of love over the idiocy of national prejudice, nor will they know the raw power of human intelligence at work on human institutions. They will hear of these things as we heard of Stalingrad and Gettysburg, as if they happened because they did. They will not know that it could have gone the other way. Peace will be as nothing to them. But there will be a difference; not something they notice every morning but something at the very bottom of things that changes everything else.

When there was peace before, it was through exhaustion, fear, or distance; war became not worth it, for one reason or another. The fighting stopped, or never started, but the fighters remained. Everyone had to be ready to fight again. There were people to be against — other people to oppose in order to *be* at all. At the bottom of every relationship, within the community and without, was a negative identity of someone else. There was no human image of self. But now that no part of ourselves must stand in opposition to who we fundamentally are, there will be a difference in who we fundamentally are. Some other dynamic will underlie us. Civilization will be another thing. Humanity in its wholeness will be something over and above its separate parts together. The political unity of all people, when it comes, will not feed the hungry or keep the peace — it may do nothing at all — but it will be a means by which these things may be done. It will not be all we hope, but it will be the hope that we have and the only future that we have. It will be what we are and the continuation of who we are into the twenty-first century and beyond.

It will be the right of Americans to preserve wild animals in Africa, and the right of Africans to preserve oil reserves in Alaska. It will be the right of Peruvians to the atmosphere over China and the right of Polynesian workers to the fruits of their labor. It will be the right of Europeans and South Africans to promote population control in India. It will be the right of North Koreans to live free from the fear of invasion. Individual lives may change little, but the collective right to subsistence, security, and environmental health will be demanded by all and assured by all.

This may seem exhausting from where we now stand. Effectiveness thins with distance: The more people cared for the less care for each. It may seem enough to cope with poverty and homelessness in one's own nation, to keep the air clean in one's own city, to defend one's own country, without taking on the world. It is enough to think of millions without thinking of billions. From where we are now, the people on Earth seem too many to manage.

But there is a beauty to the shape of the earth, a beauty that shapes the love of the earth and of its peoples. It has limits but no boundaries. It is only so large, but does not end. If you go far enough in any direction, you come back home. Concern for people who share the human condition does not end at oceans and rivers and artificial lines in the dirt but curves and resonates with distance, re-concentrating as it completes the tour. The Earth is finite but unbounded: What we manage on a united Earth will be finite, but what we care for will be unbounded. When everyone is cared for and the circle is complete, the earth and its people will be one thing. When there is no one outside the enclosure, human compassion will curve to the shape of the earth.

I believe in humanity. But as it is currently constituted, I am not proud to be human. I am not proud of what we are doing and where we are going. I will be proud to be human only when everyone is cared for. I will be proud then to be what I am.

29. The Walk

I WILL WALK FROM HERE TO THERE. IN THE STREETS AND in my mind, I will walk.

I have walked in the twentieth century. Nationalism was not a question then. I walk now in the twenty-first century, when there are questions better than any answers we have seen.

Unity will not happen at one time. There will be no culminating event. The crisis will bring the question but no answers, and we should not wait for the answers to come in. We will not know how to constitute ourselves. We will not know how capital should be controlled and by whom or how to regulate multinational corporations. We will not know how to tend the oceans and forests and atmosphere or how to spend the misspent wealth of the past. We will not know at first who will enforce the new measures, in what name, and how well they will be respected. Unity will not answer questions; it will be a means to ask them. It will be a tool, not a task. The struggle for social, environmental, and economic justice will be ongoing within it.

We will give with no assurance of what is to follow. There will be no clear path through the state of nature. There will be confusion and sacrifice for what does not yet exist. There will be losses and no clear gains. Good things will be lost. There will be trauma, shock, a hemorrhage of what we thought, a losing of the ground itself, a giving of birth. The reality of now will not survive. It will be a winning and losing of war at the same time. America will give more than most, and in so doing keep more and give less. Our self-conscious expression of self-government, our definition of government as a conscious act, our respect for what we have written of what we will do, our making of parts into a whole, our popular culture, our language — all these we will give and keep. We will hold them to ourselves and give them up finally, offering reluctantly to be ruled by them as they rule others. We will be ruled by others who are ourselves. We will fight it and have it only as we lose. There will be nothing special about America other than its uniqueness.

Unification can happen two ways. Either the parts create the whole or one of the parts becomes the whole: Either the cantons create the Swiss confederation or Prussia becomes Germany. If it happens during the era of American hegemony, the parts will create the whole. There are too many parts, and America is not strong enough to conquer them all. Neither does she care to. America did not move into Eastern Europe at the fall of the Soviet Union, as many in Russia feared or claimed they feared. America did not take Baghdad the first time. She does not want Haiti, Somalia, Bosnia, or Baghdad. This is fortunate. It is fortunate that the oceans and air are large enough to absorb what we do until we are aware of it, and that there is enough fossil fuel to give us time to learn how not to need it. It is fortunate, but it is no coincidence. It is no coincidence that we have what we need to have and that all of this is happening now.

I will walk beyond the frontiers of native altruism, past the limits of human goodness stronger than my own. But I will not walk alone.

This we demand: an immediate disassembly of all weapons of intercontinental range; an immediate destruction of all means of nuclear, biological, and chemical destructiveness; an immediate and universal ban on the international trade of any weapon or munitions; and the popular election within all existing national sovereignties, subject to the supervision of the United Nations, of representatives to a world convention for the purpose of instituting sovereign political institutions encompassing all nations — and all people — of the earth. We will walk until we get it. This is a thing more ardently to be desired than seriously to be expected.... Hearken not to the voice that petulantly tells you that the form of government recommended for your adoption is a novelty in the political world, that it has never yet had a place in the theories of the wildest projectors, that it rashly attempts what it is impossible to accomplish.... Why is the experiment of an extended republic to be rejected merely because it may comprise what is new?[31]

I will forgive myself the accidents of birth and culture. I will drink the wine on the table before me. I accept limits of wisdom and influence. I eschew the idiocy of conformity and perfection. I will walk with my friends on the path of peace and love. I will strive for justice that I cannot fulfill.

Publius

Endnotes

1   Sawyer, P. H. *From Roman Britain to Norman England.* New York: St. Martin's Press, 1978, p. 45. Quoted from Bede's "*Historia Ecclesiastica Gentis Anglorum,*" iv. 12.

2   Trevelyan, G. M. *English Social History.* New York: David McKay Co., 1942, p. 82.

3   A case can be made for tracing modern internationalism back to the Treaty of Westphalia in 1648.

4   Rossiter, Clinton, ed. *The Federalist Papers.* New York: New American Library of World Literature, 1961, p. 54.

5   Grubb, Michael. *The Kyoto Protocol: A Guide and Assessments.* The Royal Institute of International Affairs, London, 1999, pp. 7–13.

6   Ely, Northcutt, Washington, D.C., attorney, in *The Law of the Sea: U.S. Interests and Alternatives.* Washington, D.C.: American Enterprise Institute for Public Policy Research, 1976. Another speaker at the same forum (pp. 38–39) stated that the cost–benefit ratio for double-hull, segregated ballast oil tankers that might be required by the Convention was 20 to 1 — that is, costs far exceeded environmental "benefits."

7   Sklair, Leslie. *Assembling for Development.* Boston: Unwin Hyman, 1989, pp. 62–63.

8   Ibid., p. 95.

9   Biomass would not have to be "burned" in the common sense of the word. Most likely, it would be converted to alcohol and used in fuel cells to heat houses, power vehicles, and generate electricity.

10 Commager, Henry Steele, and Richard B. Morris, eds. *The Spirit of Seventy-Six.* New York: Bobbs-Merrill, Vol. I, p. 82.

11 Ibid., p. 71.

12 Ibid., p. 83.

13 Nevins, Allan. *The American States During and After the Revolution, 1775–1789.* New York: Macmillan Company, 1924, pp. 578–582.

14 Bellesiles, Michael A. *Revolutionary Outlaws: Ethan Allen and the Struggle for Independence on the Early American Frontier.* Charlottesville: University of Virginia Press, 1993, p. 179.

15 Taylor, Robert J. *The Susquehannah Company Papers,* Wyoming Historical and Geological Society. Ithaca: Cornell University Press, 1968, Vol. VI, pp. 422–423. Extract from the *Connecticut Courant*, January 22, 1776, attributed to Colonel Zebulun Butler, commander of the Connecticut militia in Wyoming Valley, against the Plunkett Expedition from Pennsylvania.

16 Nevins, pp. 583–650.

17 Levy, Leonard W. *Essays on the Making of the Constitution.* New York: Oxford University Press, 1969, p. 194.

18 Ibid., p. 194.

19 McMaster, John Bach, and Frederick D. Stone. *Pennsylvania and the Federal Constitution 1787–1788.* New York: Da Capo Press, 1970, pp. 486–487. Written in the *Independent Gazetteer* by "One of the People."

20 Ibid., p. 493. Eyewitness writer to *Independent Gazeteer*, January 1, 1788.

21 Brunhouse, Robert L. *The Counter-Revolution in Pennsylvania, 1776–1790.* Harrisburg: Pennsylvania Historical Commission, 1942, pp. 210–211.

22 McMaster, p. 496. From Petition to the Executive Council of the State of Pennsylvania, February 13, 1788.

23 Rossiter, p. 42.

24 Zobel, Hiller B. *The Boston Massacre.* New York: W.W. Norton, 1970, p. 29. Much of the following account is from Zobel's book.

25 Dalton, Dennis. *Mahatma Gandhi: Non-violent Power in Action.* New York: Columbia University Press, 1993, p. 133.

26 Fischer, Louis, ed. *The Essential Gandhi: An Anthology of His Writings on His Life, Works, and Ideas.* New York: Vintage Books, 1962, pp. 262–264.

27 Deats, Richard. *Martin Luther King, Jr., Spirit-Led Prophet: A Biography.* New York: New City Press, 2000, p. 28.

28 Patterson, Lillie. *Martin Luther King, Jr. and the Freedom Movement: Makers of America.* New York: Facts on File, 1989, p. 110.

29 Hoobler, Dorothy, and Thomas Hoobler. *Mandela: The Man, the Struggle, the Triumph.* New York: Franklin Watts, 1992, p. 53.

30 Bell, Dick, and Michael Renner. "A New Marshall Plan? Advancing Human Security and Controlling Terrorism." Washington, D.C.: Worldwatch Institute, October 9, 2001, and World Game Institute, "Global Priorities," wall chart, at www.worldgame.org, 2002.

31 Rossiter, pp. 33, 42, 47 (Hamilton), and 104 (Madison).